BIBLE
QUESTIONS
& ANSWERS

COLLECTIONS 1 AND 2

Written by Vickie Save
Illustrated by Ken Save

BARBOUR
PUBLISHING, INC.
Uhrichsville, Ohio

ISBN 1-55748-997-1

Published by Barbour Publishing, Inc., P.O. Box 719, Uhrichsville, Ohio 44683
http://www.barbourbooks.com

ecpa Member of the
Evangelical Christian
Publishers Association

Printed in the United States of America.

"_ _ _ _ _ IS THE PERSON WHO DOESN'T _ _ _ _ _ _ _ TO THE WICKED. HE DOESN'T GO WHERE _ _ _ _ _ _ _ GO. HE DOESN'T DO WHAT _ _ _ PEOPLE DO. HE LOVES THE _ _ _ _ _ TEACHINGS. HE THINKS ABOUT THOSE

_ _ _ _ _ _ _ _ _ _ _ AND _ _ _ _ _ _!"

PSALM 1:1-2

WORD LIST

TEACHINGS	LISTEN
BAD	DAY
NIGHT	SINNERS
HAPPY	LORD'S

HOW MUCH OF THE BIBLE DO YOU KNOW

MATCH THE ANSWERS ON THE FOLLOWING PAGE TO THE QUESTIONS BELOW.

1. WHO SAID, "I AM WHO I AM"?

   EXODUS 3:14

   _____

2. WHAT DID GOD CREATE ON THE FIRST DAY

   GENESIS 1:3-5

   _____

3. WHO BUILT THE ARK?

   GENESIS 6:13-1

   _____

4. HOW MANY SONS DID NOAH HAVE?

   GENESIS 6:10

   _____

5. WHAT WERE THE NAMES OF NOAH'S SONS

   GENESIS 6:10

   _____   _____   _____

6. WHO SAID, "AM I SUPPOSED TO TAKE CARE OF MY BROTHER?"

   GENESIS 4:9

   _____

LIGHT	HAM
SHEM	JOSEPH
MOSES	NOAH
SIX	JAPHETH
GOD	CAIN
THREE	SEA

MULTIPLE CHOICE

CIRCLE THE CORRECT ANSWER.

1. WHOSE LIFE WAS SAVED BY BEING LOWER OVER A WALL IN A BASKET?

   ACTS 9:25

   A. JOHN'S

   B. THE CRIPPLED MAN

   C. SAUL'S

2. DAVID SAID THAT GOD MADE MAN A LITTLE LOWER THAN WHAT?

   PSALM 8:5

   A. STARS

   B. ANGELS

   C. ANIMALS

3. WHERE WAS MOSES STANDING WHEN GOD TOLD HIM TO TAKE OFF HIS SHOES?

   EXODUS 3:5

   A. ON A MOUNTAIN

   B. ON HOLY GROUND

CONT'D ON NEXT PAGE...

4

HOW MANY DISCIPLES HAD THE NAME
OF JAMES ?

MATTHEW 10:2-3

        A. TWO

        B. FOUR

        C. SEVEN

WHAT DOES THE HEBREW WORD, "ABBA ,"
MEAN ?

ROMANS 8:15

        A. HELLO

        B. DADDY

        C. MOMMY

WHO DID JESUS SAY THE SABBATH
WAS MADE FOR ?

MARK 2:27

        A. GOD

        B. UNBELIEVERS

        C. MAN

MATCH THE ANSWERS

MATCH THE ANSWERS ON THE FOLLOWING
PAGE TO THE QUESTIONS BELOW.

1. WHO ASKED GOD TO SPARE SODOM?

   _____
   GENESIS 18:23-3?

2. WHO WROTE FIRST AND SECOND CORINTHIAN

   _____
   1 COR.1:1 , 2 COR.1:?

3. WHO DID JESUS SAY WILL INHERIT THE
   EARTH?
   MATTHEW 5:5

   _____

4. WHAT IS THE NAME GIVEN TO JESUS
   THAT MEANS "GOD IS WITH US"?
   MATTHEW 1:23

   _____

5. WHAT WILL GOD GIVE US PLENTY OF IF
   WE ASK HIM?
   JAMES 1:5

   _____

6. WHERE IN EGYPT DID JOSEPH'S
   FAMILY LIVE?
   GENESIS 47:6

   _____

THE STRONG   PAUL

PETER   EMMANUEL

HOSANNA   ABRAHAM

MONEY   WISDOM

GOSHEN   THE MEEK

7

MULTIPLE CHOICE

CIRCLE THE CORRECT ANSWER.

1. WHAT WAS SARAH'S NAME BEFORE
GOD CHANGED IT ?

GENESIS 17:1

    A. SALLY

    B. HAGAR

    C. SARAI

2. WHO DID PAUL CALL HIS OWN SON ?

1 TIMOTHY 1:1-2

    A. PETER

    B. TIMOTHY

    C. JOHN

3. WHO PREACHED ON THE DAY OF
PENTECOST ?

ACTS 2:14

    A. JOHN

    B. PAUL

    C. PETER

CONT'D ON NEXT PAGE...

WHAT DID JACOB WEAR TO TRICK HIS
FATHER?

GENESIS 27:15-24

    A. SHEEPSKIN

    B. BEARSKIN

    C. GOATSKIN

HOW MANY PLAGUES DID GOD BRING
ON EGYPT?

EXODUS 7-11

    A. SEVEN

    B. TEN

    C. TWELVE

WHAT WAS THE NAME OF THE WELL THAT
THE SAMARITAN WOMAN DREW WATER
FROM?

JOHN 4:6-7

    A. SAMARIA WELL

    B. JOSEPH'S WELL

    C. JACOB'S WELL

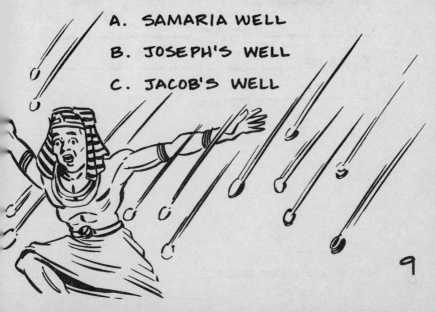

9

FILL IN THE BLANKS

WORD LIST

LIFE   RESURRECTION

FOOL   WICKED

LORD   SHEPHERD

EVERYTHING   NEED

1. IN JOHN 11: 25, JESUS SAID, " I AM
   THE _ _ _ _ _ _ _ _ _ _ _ _ _
   AND THE _ _ _ _ . "

2. IN PSALM 14:1 , IT SAYS ,"A
   _ _ _ _ _ _ _ _ _ _ SAYS
   TO HIMSELF, 'THERE IS NO GOD'. "

3. IN PSALM 23:1 , IT SAYS , " THE
   _ _ _ _ IS MY _ _ _ _ _ _ _ _
   I HAVE _ _ _ _ _ _ _ _ _ _ _
   I _ _ _ _ . "

FILL IN THE BLANKS

WORD LIST

LIGHT	CREATED	FEMALE
SAVES	IMAGE	
PROTECTS	AFRAID	
WAY	TRUTH	
LIFE	MALE	

IN PSALM 27:1, IT SAYS, " THE LORD
IS MY _ _ _ _ _ AND THE
ONE WHO _ _ _ _ _ ME. I
FEAR NO ONE. THE LORD
_ _ _ _ _ _ _ _ MY LIFE.
I AM _ _ _ _ _ _ OF NO ONE."

. IN JOHN 14:6, JESUS SAID, "I AM THE
_ _ _ . I AM THE _ _ _ _ _
AND THE _ _ _ _ ."

. IN GENESIS 1:27, IT SAYS ," SO GOD
_ _ _ _ _ _ _ HUMAN BEINGS IN
HIS _ _ _ _ _ . IN THE IMAGE OF
GOD HE CREATED THEM. HE CREATED
THEM _ _ _ _ AND _ _ _ _ _ _ ."

11

MATCH THE ANSWERS

MATCH THE ANSWERS ON THE
FOLLOWING PAGE TO THE QUESTIONS
BELOW.

1. WHO WAS ISHMAEL'S MOTHER?

GENESIS 16:15

_____

2. WHO WAS THE FATHER OF MANY NATIONS

GENESIS 17:1-4

_____

3. WHO WAS THE BROTHER OF MARTHA
AND MARY?

JOHN 11:1-2

_____

4. WHAT IS THE ROOT OF ALL EVIL?

1 TIMOTHY 6:10

_____

5. WHAT IS THE JEWISH DAY OF REST
CALLED?

EXODUS 20:10

_____

6. IN WHAT AREA IS BETHLEHEM
LOCATED?

MATTHEW 2:1

_____

12

SARAH	ABRAHAM
ISAAC	SELFISHNESS
LOVE OF MONEY	HAGAR
LAZARUS	PETER
JERUSALEM	SABBATH
SUNDAY	JUDEA

MULTIPLE CHOICE

CIRCLE THE CORRECT ANSWER.

1. WHAT WAS THE NAME OF ABRAHAM'S PROMISED SON? GENESIS 21:3

    A. ISHMAEL

    B. RONALD

    C. ISAAC

2. WHAT WAS THE NAME OF JACOB'S YOUNGEST SON? GENESIS 35:18

    A. JOSEPH

    B. JUDAH

    C. BENJAMIN

3. WHO DID AQUILA AND PRISCILLA MEET IN CORINTH? ACTS 18:1-2

    A. JOHN

    B. PAUL

    C. PETER

CONT'D ON NEXT PAGE...

WHAT DID KING BELSHAZZAR SEE ON THE ?

DANIEL 5:5-8

    A. FINGER PRINTS

    B. A HAND WRITING

    C. A BUG

. WHAT DID GOD MAKE GROW OVER JONAH TO GIVE HIM SHADE ?

JONAH 4:6

    A. A HOUSE

    B. A TREE

    C. A VINE

. WHERE DID KING SOLOMON FIND CEDAR TREES FOR THE TEMPLE ?

1 KINGS 5:6

    A. A LUMBER STORE

    B. HIS BACK YARD

    C. LEBANON

MULTIPLE CHOICE

CIRCLE THE CORRECT ANSWER.

1. HOW MANY BOOKS ARE THERE IN THE BIBLE?

   A. SIXTY-EIGHT

   B. SIXTY-SIX

   C. THIRTY-FOUR

2. WHAT COMMANDMENT SAYS, "YOU MUST NOT MURDER ANYONE"?

   EXODUS 20:13

   A. TWELFTH

   B. SIXTH

   C. SEVENTH

3. HOW MANY BOOKS ARE IN THE NEW TESTAMENT?

   A. TWENTY-SIX

   B. TWENTY-EIGHT

   C. TWENTY-SEVEN

CONT'D ON NEXT PAGE...

HOW MANY FRIENDS CAME TO SPEAK
WITH JOB?   JOB 2:11

    A. ONE

    B. THREE

    C. THIRTY-SIX

5. ON WHICH DAY DID GOD CREATE THE
SUN, MOON, AND STARS?   GENESIS 1:14-19

    A. SECOND

    B. FOURTH

    C. SIXTH

6. HOW MANY TIMES DID JESUS ASK
PETER IF HE LOVED HIM?   JOHN 21: 15-17

    A. ONE

    B. THREE

    C. FIVE

17

FILL IN THE BLANKS

WORD LIST

PATIENT	TRUST	ANGRY
JEALOUS	RUDE	HOPES
TRUTH	SELFISH	WRONGS
BRAG	STRONG	HAPPY
PROUD	KIND	

" LOVE IS _ _ _ _ _ _ _ AND

_ _ _ _ _ . LOVE IS NOT _ _ _ _ _ _ _ _

IT DOES NOT _ _ _ _ _ , AND IT IS NOT

_ _ _ _ _ _ . LOVE IS NOT _ _ _ _ _ ,

IT IS NOT _ _ _ _ _ _ _ _ , AND

DOES NOT BECOME _ _ _ _ _ _

EASILY. LOVE DOES NOT REMEMBER

_ _ _ _ _ _ _ DONE AGAINST IT.

LOVE IS NOT _ _ _ _ _ _ WITH

EVIL , BUT IS HAPPY WITH

_ _ _ _ _ _ .

CONT'D NEXT PAGE...

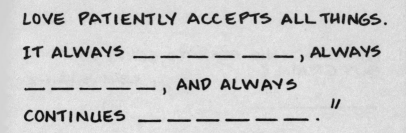

LOVE PATIENTLY ACCEPTS ALL THINGS.
IT ALWAYS _ _ _ _ _ _, ALWAYS
_ _ _ _ _ _, AND ALWAYS
CONTINUES _ _ _ _ _ _. "

1 CORINTHIANS 13: 4-7

THIS IS LOVE

MATCH THE ANSWERS

MATCH THE ANSWERS ON THE FOLLOWING PAGE TO THE QUESTIONS BELOW.

1. WHO SENT HIS SONS TO EGYPT TO BUY GRAIN ?

   GENESIS 42:1-2

   _____

2. WHO SAID TO JESUS, " YOU ARE THE CHRIST, THE SON OF THE LIVING GOD " ?

   MATTHEW 16:16

   _____

3. WHO SAID, " WHEN I NEEDED CLOTHES, YOU CLOTHED ME " ?

   MATTHEW 25:36

   _____

4. HOW MANY BOOKS IN THE BIBLE ARE NAMED "JOHN" ?

   _____

5. ON WHICH DAY DID GOD CREATE THE ANIMALS OF THE WATER AND THE AIR?

   GENESIS 1:20-23

   _____

6. WHAT ARE THE STORIES CALLED THAT JESUS TAUGHT BY ?

   MATTHEW 13:13

   _____

FOUR   JOHN

PETER   ISAAC

JAMES   JESUS

JACOB   THREE

SIXTH   FIFTH

TALES   PARABLES

MATCH THE ANSWERS

MATCH THE ANSWERS ON THE FOLLOWING PAGE TO THE QUESTIONS BELOW.

1. WHO SOLD HIS BIRTHRIGHT ?

_____   GENESIS 25:32-33

2. WHO WAS JACOB TRICKED INTO MARRYING ?

GENESIS 29:23-25

_____

3. WHAT OLD TESTAMENT COUPLE HAD TWIN SONS ?

GENESIS 25:20-24

_____

4. WHOSE DAUGHTER DANCED AT HEROD'S BIRTHDAY PARTY ?

MATTHEW 14:6

_____

5. WHAT DID SOLOMON HAVE SEVEN HUNDRED OF ?

1 KINGS 11:3

_____

6. ON THE ROAD TO WHAT CITY DID THE GOOD SAMARITAN HELP THE BEATEN MAN ?

LUKE 10:30-33

_____

RACHEL

NEW YORK

ESAU

HERODIAS'

KIDS

ABRAHAM
& SARAH

LEAH

ELIZABETH

REUBEN

WIVES

JERICHO

ISAAC
& REBEKAH

653...

MULTIPLE CHOICE

CIRCLE THE CORRECT ANSWER.

1. WHO WAS MOSES' WIFE?

   EXODUS 2:21

   A. HAGAR

   B. ZIPPORAH

   C. REBEKAH

2. WHO WAS THE FIRST PRIEST OF ISRAEL?

   EXODUS 28:3

   A. ABRAHAM

   B. MOSES

   C. AARON

3. WHO WAS A JUDGE FOR THE PEOPLE OF ISRAEL FOR TWENTY YEARS?

   JUDGES 16:31

   A. SAUL

   B. SAMSON

   C. DAVID

CONT'D NEXT PAGE...

CONT'D FROM PREVIOUS PAGE.

WHO PREACHED IN THE WILDERNESS OF
JUDEA? MATTHEW 3:1

    A. JOHN

    B. JESUS

    C. JOHN THE BAPTIST

WHAT WAS THE NAME OF MARY'S SISTER
WHO WORKED HARD IN THE KITCHEN?
LUKE 10:40

    A. RUTH

    B. DEBORAH

    C. MARTHA

5. WHO WROTE THE BOOK OF REVELATION?
REVELATION 1:4

    A. PAUL

    B. JOHN

    C. PETER

MATCH THE ANSWERS

MATCH THE ANSWERS ON THE FOLLOWING PAGE TO THE QUESTIONS BELOW.

1. HOW OLD WAS ABRAHAM WHEN ISAAC WAS BORN?

   GENESIS 21:5

   _____

2. HOW MANY DAYS WAS SAUL BLIND?

   ACTS 9:9

   _____

3. WHAT COMMANDMENT IS "HONOR YOUR FATHER AND YOUR MOTHER"?

   EXODUS 20:12

   _____

4. WHAT DOES "GENESIS" MEAN?

   _____

5. WHAT LANGUAGE WAS THE NEW TESTAMENT WRITTEN IN?

   _____

6. WHAT NEW TESTAMENT BOOK TELLS OF JESUS GOING UP TO HEAVEN?

   _____

END   EIGHTH

FOURTH   THREE

EIGHTY   BEGINNING

FIFTH   ONE HUNDRED

GREEK   ENGLISH

ACTS   JOHN

FILL IN THE BLANKS

WORD LIST

STAND   DOOR

KNOCK   ANYONE

VOICE   OPENS

EAT   HE

"HERE I AM! I _ _ _ _ _ AT THE _ _ _ _ AND _ _ _ _ _. IF _ _ _ _ _ _ HEARS MY _ _ _ _ _ AND _ _ _ _ _ THE DOOR, I WILL COME IN AND _ _ _ WITH HIM. AND _ _ WILL EAT WITH ME."

REVELATION 3:20

28

FILL IN THE BLANKS

WORD LIST

ASK   KNOCK

SEARCH   OPEN

FIND   GOD

YOU   DOOR

"CONTINUE TO _ _ _ AND _ _ _ WILL GIVE TO YOU. CONTINUE TO _ _ _ _ _ _ AND _ _ _ WILL _ _ _ _. CONTINUE TO _ _ _ _ _ AND THE _ _ _ _ WILL BE _ _ _ _ FOR YOU."

MATTHEW 7:7

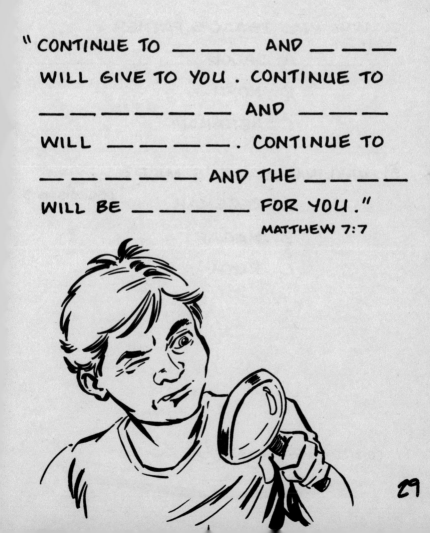

MULTIPLE CHOICE

CIRCLE THE CORRECT ANSWER.

1. WHO WAS TAKEN OUT OF SODOM BEFORE IT WAS DESTROYED ?

    GENESIS 19:15

    A. ABRAHAM AND HIS FAMILY

    B. LOT AND HIS FAMILY

    C. ISAAC AND HIS FAMILY

2. WHO WAS ISAAC'S FATHER ?

    GENESIS 21:3

    A. JACOB

    B. NOAH

    C. ABRAHAM

3. WHO WAS SARAI'S MAID?

    GENESIS 16:3

    A. REBEKAH

    B. HAGAR

    C. RUTH

CONT'D NEXT PAGE...

JESUS RAISED LAZARUS FROM THE DEAD.
WHO WERE LAZARUS' SISTERS?

JOHN 11: 1-3

    A. MARY AND ELIZABETH

    B. RUTH AND NAOMI

    C. MARTHA AND MARY

. WHAT DID JESUS SAY HE WOULD BUILD
HIS CHURCH ON?

MATTHEW 16: 18

    A. THIS MOUNTAIN

    B. THIS HILL

    C. THIS ROCK

5. WHAT DID JUDAS DO AFTER HE BETRAYED
JESUS ?

MATTHEW 27: 5

    A. SAID SORRY

    B. CRIED

    C. HANGED HIMSELF

MULTIPLE CHOICE

CIRCLE THE CORRECT ANSWER.

1. WHAT DOES TESTAMENT MEAN ?

   A. TO TEST

   B. AGREEMENT

   C. BOOKS

2. WHAT DID THE ISRAELITES PUT ON THEIR DOOR POSTS SO THAT THE DEATH ANGEL WOULD PASS BY ?

   EXODUS 12 : 21 : 23

   A. GOAT'S BLOOD

   B. PAINT

   C. LAMB'S BLOOD

3. WHAT ARE WE TO POUR ON THE SICK SO THAT THE PRAYER OF FAITH WILL MAKE THEM WELL ?

   JAMES 5:14

   A. MEDICINE

   B. WATER

   C. OIL

CONT'D NEXT PAGE...

WHAT ARE WE SUPPOSED TO DO WHEN
WE SIN ?

JAMES 5:16

    A. FORGET ABOUT IT

    B. CONFESS IT TO EACH OTHER

    C. PRETEND IT DIDN'T HAPPEN

JESUS CALLED MATTHEW TO BE A DISCIPLE.
WHAT WAS HE BEFORE JESUS CALLED HIM?

    A. A FISHERMAN   MATTHEW 9:9

    B. A TAX COLLECTOR

    C. A BASEBALL PLAYER

WHAT DID JESUS SAY HE WOULD MAKE
PETER AND ANDREW ?

MARK 1:16-17

    A. SINGERS

    B. KINGS

    C. FISHERS OF MEN

MATCH THE ANSWERS

MATCH THE ANSWERS ON THE FOLLOWING PAGE TO THE QUESTIONS BELOW.

1. IN THE ARMOR OF GOD, WHAT IS THE SHIELD CALLED?
   EPHESIANS 6:16

   _____

2. WHAT IS THE HELMET CALLED?
   EPHESIANS 6:17

   _____

3. WHAT IS THE SWORD CALLED?
   EPHESIANS 6:17

   _____

4. WHAT IS THE BELT CALLED?
   EPHESIANS 6:14

   _____

5. WHAT INGREDIENT IN THE KITCHEN DID JESUS SAY WE WERE LIKE?
   MATTHEW 5:13

   _____

6. WHAT BOOK OF THE BIBLE HAS THE MOST CHAPTERS?

   _____

SALVATION   PROTECTION

WORD OF GOD   SPIRIT

FAITH   DOUBT

SUGAR   TRUTH

HALF TRUTH   SALT

PROVERBS   PSALMS

3S

MATCH THE ANSWERS

MATCH THE ANSWERS ON THE FOLLOWING PAGE TO THE QUESTIONS BELOW.

1. IN THE DESERT, GOD GAVE THE ISRAELIT MANNA TO EAT. WHAT ELSE DID GOD GIVE THEM?

   EXODUS 16:13

   _____

2. WHAT DOES JESUS GIVE TO THOSE WHO CHOOSE TO FOLLOW HIM?

   JOHN 10:27-28

   _____

3. WHAT SPECIAL DAY WAS IT WHEN THE BELIEVERS RECEIVED THE HOLY SPIRIT?

   ACTS 2:1-4

   _____

4. A MAN REAPS WHAT HE ... WHAT?

   GALATIANS 6:7

   _____

5. WHAT DID JESUS SAY HE HAD OVERCOME

   JOHN 16:33

   _____

6. IN WHAT COUNTRY DID ISAAC FIND A WIFE?

   GENESIS 24:4,10

   _____

36

ETERNAL LIFE   EARTH
QUAILS   CHICKEN
EASTER   CANDY
EATS   PENTECOST
WORLD   SOWS
MAGOG   MESOPOTAMIA

FILL IN THE BLANKS

" _ _ _ _ _ SAID, ' A

_ _ _ _ _ _ DOES NOT

_ _ _ _ ONLY BY _ _ _ _ _

_ _ _ _ _ _ . BUT A PERSON

LIVES _ _ _ _ _ _ _ _ _ _ _

THE _ _ _ _ SAYS. ' "

MATTHEW 4:4

FILL IN THE BLANKS

WORD LIST

BEGINS	RESPECT
WISDOM	LORD
KNOWLEDGE	FOOLISH
SELF-CONTROL	

"_ _ _ _ _ _ _ _ _ _

_ _ _ _ _ _ _ WITH

_ _ _ _ _ _ _ _ FOR THE

_ _ _ _ _ . BUT _ _ _ _ _ _ _ _

PEOPLE HATE _ _ _ _ _ _ _ AND

_ _ _ _ - _ _ _ _ _ _ _ _ ."

PROVERBS 1:7

39

FILL IN THE BLANKS

WORD LIST

LOVE   KINDNESS

JOY   FAITHFULNESS

SELF-CONTROL PEACE

GENTLENESS   PATIENCE

GOODNESS

" BUT THE SPIRIT GIVES ____ ,

____ , ____ ,

____ ,

____ ,

____ ,

____

____ ,

AND ____ -

____ . THERE IS

NO LAW THAT SAYS THESE THINGS

ARE WRONG. "

GALATIANS 5:22-23

FILL IN THE BLANKS

WORD LIST

HELPER	EVERYTHING
NAME	YOU
HOLY	REMEMBER
FATHER	HE

" BUT THE _ _ _ _ _ _ WILL

TEACH YOU _ _ _ _ _ _ _ _ _ _.

_ _ WILL CAUSE YOU TO

_ _ _ _ _ _ _ _ ALL THE

THINGS I TOLD _ _ _. THIS

HELPER IS THE _ _ _ _ SPIRIT

WHOM THE _ _ _ _ _ _ WILL

SEND IN MY _ _ _ _."

JOHN 14:26

41

MATCH THE ANSWERS

MATCH THE ANSWERS ON THE FOLLOWING
PAGE TO THE QUESTIONS BELOW.

1. IN THE PARABLE OF THE TALENTS, HOW
   MANY SERVANTS WERE GIVEN TALENTS ?

   _____   MATTHEW 25:14-15

2. HOW OLD WAS JAIRUS' DAUGHTER WHEN
   SHE GOT SICK ?   LUKE 8:42

   _____

3. HOW MANY WARNINGS, OR "WOES", DID
   JESUS GIVE TO THE PHARISEES ?

   _____   MATTHEW 23:13-36

4. HOW MANY WIVES DID JACOB HAVE?

   _____   GENESIS 29:24-30
                                     30:4,9

5. HOW MANY PIECES OF SILVER WAS JUDAS
   PAID TO BETRAY JESUS ?

   _____   MATTHEW 26:15

6. HOW MANY CONCUBINES DID KING
   SOLOMON HAVE ?   1 KINGS 11:3

   _____

NINE	EIGHT
FOUR	THREE
TWELVE	TEN
FIVE	SEVEN
THIRTY	ONE HUNDRED
ONE THOUSAND	THREE HUNDRED

43

MATCH THE ANSWERS

MATCH THE ANSWERS ON THE FOLLOWING PAGE TO THE QUESTIONS BELOW.

1. HOW MANY WERE AT THE LAST SUPPER WITH JESUS?

   MATTHEW 26: 19-20

   _____

2. HOW LONG IS A MILLENIUM?

   REVELATION 20: 4, 6-7

   _____

3. WHICH OLD TESTAMENT BOOK TELLS ABOUT THE LIFE OF ABRAHAM?

   _____

4. WHAT PEOPLE WANTED TO KNOW THE SECRET OF SAMSON'S STRENGTH?

   JUDGES 16: 4-5

   _____

5. WHO WAS THE ONLY FEMALE JUDGE OF ISRAEL?

   JUDGES 4: 4-14

   _____

6. THE LORD SAID HE IS THE ALPHA AND THE OMEGA. WHAT DOES OMEGA MEAN?

   REVELATION 22: 13

   _____

TEN THOUSAND YEARS   PHILISTINES

EXODUS   ISRAELITES

ELEVEN   TWELVE

RUTH   LAST, END

FIRST, BEGINNING   DEBORAH

GENESIS   ONE THOUSAND YEARS

MULTIPLE CHOICE

CIRCLE THE CORRECT ANSWER.

1. WHO WAS JOSEPH'S MOTHER?

   GENESIS 30:22-24

   A. LEAH

   B. RACHEL

   C. REBEKAH

2. WHO WAS THE FIRST KING OF ISRAEL?

   1 SAMUEL 10:21-25

   A. AARON

   B. DAVID

   C. SAUL

3. WHAT WAS BELTESHAZZAR'S OTHER NAME?

   DANIEL 1:7

   A. SIMON

   B. DANIEL

   C. JOB

CONT'D NEXT PAGE...

4. WHO WAS THE COUSIN OF MORDECAI
THAT BECAME A QUEEN?   ESTHER 2:15-17

      A. RUTH

      B. NAOMI

      C. ESTHER

5. WHO WROTE THE RIDDLE ABOUT
THE LION?   JUDGES 14:16-18

      A. JUDGES

      B. SOLOMON

      C. SAMSON

6. WHO CALLED DOWN FIRE FROM
HEAVEN?   2 KINGS 1:10

      A. ELISHA

      B. ELIJAH

      C. JEREMIAH

MULTIPLE CHOICE

CIRCLE THE CORRECT ANSWER.

1. WHAT EXCUSE DID MOSES GIVE TO GOD FOR WHY HE DIDN'T WANT TO GO TO EGYPT?

   A. "I'M TOO TIRED." EXODUS 4:10-16

   B. "I MADE OTHER PLANS."

   C. "I AM SLOW TO SPEAK."

2. WHAT DID JOSEPH INTERPRET FOR PHARAOH?

   GENESIS 41:14-36

   A. HIS WIFE'S DREAMS

   B. A RECIPE FOR PUDDING

   C. HIS DREAMS

3. JESUS SAID THAT WHEN HE RETURNS AGAIN, HE WILL COME LIKE A...WHAT?

   REVELATION 16:15

   A. FLASH OF LIGHTNING

   B. BOLT OF THUNDER

   C. THIEF IN THE NIGHT

CONT'D NEXT PAGE...

WHAT DID THE WOMEN BRING TO
JESUS' TOMB?

MARK 16:1

    A. FLOWERS

    B. SWEET SPICES

    C. PEOPLE

WHAT DID ESAU DO FOR A LIVING?

GENESIS 25:27

    A. FARM

    B. BUILD

    C. HUNT

IN THE PARABLE OF THE SOWER, WHAT
DOES THE SEED STAND FOR?

LUKE 8:11

    A. A PLANT

    B. CORN

    C. THE WORD OF GOD

MULTIPLE CHOICE

CIRCLE THE CORRECT ANSWER.

1. WHAT DID JESUS TELL THE DISCIPLES TO DO IF THEY WERE NOT WELCOME AT SOMEONE'S HOME?

   MATTHEW 10:14

   A. GET ANGRY.

   B. WHINE AND CRY.

   C. SHAKE THE DUST OFF YOUR FEET.

2. WHAT WAS JOHN THE BAPTIST'S CLOTHING MADE OF?

   MATTHEW 3:4

   A. SILK

   B. WOOL

   C. CAMEL'S HAIR

3. WHAT KIND OF CROWN WILL JESUS GIVE US IF WE ARE FAITHFUL TO THE END?

   REVELATION 2:10

   A. CROWN OF GOLD

   B. CROWN OF SILVER

   C. CROWN OF LIFE

CONT'D NEXT PAGE...

WHAT ARE WE TOLD TO TAKE UP TO FOLLOW JESUS?

MATTHEW 10:38

A. OUR SUITCASES

B. OUR CROSSES

C. OUR COATS

FAITH WITHOUT WHAT IS DEAD?

JAMES 2:20

A. WORDS

B. WORKS

C. WISDOM

WHAT DID DANIEL AND HIS FRIENDS REFUSE TO EAT AND DRINK AT THE KING'S TABLE?

DANIEL 1:8

A. LIVER, ONIONS, AND CARROT JUICE

B. MEAT AND WINE

C. PIZZA AND SODA

FILL IN THE BLANKS

WORD LIST

TRUST	EVERYTHING
SUCCESS	OWN
HEART	REMEMBER
DEPEND	LORD

" _ _ _ _ _ IN THE _ _ _ _ _
WITH ALL YOUR _ _ _ _ _. DON'T
_ _ _ _ _ _ ON YOUR _ _ _
UNDERSTANDING. _ _ _ _ _ _ _ _ _
THE LORD IN _ _ _ _ _ _ _ _ _ _
YOU DO. AND HE WILL GIVE YOU
_ _ _ _ _ _ _ "

PROVERBS 3:5-6

FILL IN THE BLANKS

WORD LIST

DEPEND	SUN
NOONDAY	LORD
FAIRNESS	GOODNESS
HE	CARE

" _ _ _ _ _ _ ON THE _ _ _ _ .
TRUST HIM AND _ _ WILL TAKE
_ _ _ _ _ OF YOU . THEN YOUR
_ _ _ _ _ _ _ _ WILL
SHINE LIKE THE _ _ _ . YOUR
_ _ _ _ _ _ _ _ WILL SHINE
LIKE THE _ _ _ _ _ _ _ SUN. "

PSALM 37:5-6

53

FILL IN THE BLANKS

" _ _ _ _ AND _ _ _ _ _ THE _ _ _ _ . DON'T BE _ _ _ _ _ _ WHEN OTHERS GET _ _ _ _ OR WHEN SOMEONE ELSE'S PLANS SUCCEED. DON'T GET _ _ _ _ _ _ . DON'T BE UPSET; IT ONLY _ _ _ _ _ TO _ _ _ _ _ _ _ . "

PSALM 37:7-8

FILL IN THE BLANKS

WORD LIST

EAT   ROARING

CAREFUL   CONTROL

DEVIL   LOOKING

HE   ENEMY

" _ _ _ _ _ _ _ YOURSELVES
AND BE _ _ _ _ _ _ _ .
THE _ _ _ _ _ IS YOUR
_ _ _ _ _ . AND _ _ GOES
AROUND LIKE A _ _ _ _ _ _ _
LION _ _ _ _ _ _ _ FOR
SOMEONE TO _ _ _ ."

1 PETER 5:8

YUM!
— YUM!

55

MATCH THE ANSWERS

MATCH THE ANSWERS ON THE FOLLOWING PAGE TO THE QUESTIONS BELOW.

1. WHO DID ISAAC BLESS INSTEAD OF ESAU?

   GENESIS 27: 21-23

   _____

2. WHO TOLD THE BROTHERS OF JOSEPH NOT TO HARM JOSEPH?

   GENESIS 37:22

   _____

3. WHO SAID THEY SHOULD SELL JOSEPH RATHER THAN KILL HIM?

   GENESIS 37: 26-27

   _____

4. WHO HAD A DREAM ABOUT THE SUN, MOON, AND STARS BOWING DOWN TO HIM?

   GENESIS 37: 5-9

   _____

5. WHO PURCHASED JOSEPH AS A SLAVE?

   GENESIS 37:36

   _____

6. WHO WAS JOSEPH'S MOTHER?

   GENESIS 30:22-24

   _____

LEAH   RACHEL

BENJAMIN   JACOB

JUDAH   REUBEN

PONTIUS PILATE   POTIPHAR

SAMSON   JOSEPH

ZIPPORAH   JOB

MATCH THE ANSWERS

MATCH THE ANSWERS ON THE FOLLOWING PAGE TO THE QUESTIONS BELOW.

1. WHO WAS THE FATHER OF JAMES AND JOHN?

   LUKE 5:10

   _____

2. WHAT TWO DISCIPLES FOLLOWED JESUS FIRST?

   MATTHEW 4:18

   _____

3. HOW MANY BOOKS IN THE NEW TESTAMENT HAVE ONLY ONE CHAPTER?

   _____

4. THE FOUR GOSPELS ARE ABOUT WHOM?

   _____

5. WHAT DO WE CALL THE DAY IN WHICH WE REMEMBER JESUS' DEATH ON THE CROSS?

   _____

6. WHICH DISCIPLE WAS SENT TO THE ISLAND OF PATMOS?

   REVELATION 1:9

   _____

FOUR	JOHN
JOHN THE BAPTIST	MATTHEW & JOHN
EASTER	ZEBEDEE
ZECHARIAH	THREE
PAUL	JESUS
GOOD FRIDAY	SIMON PETER & ANDREW

MULTIPLE CHOICE

CIRCLE THE CORRECT ANSWER.

1. ON WHAT WAS JOHN THE BAPTIST'S HEAD PUT TO GIVE TO HERODIAS' DAUGHTER?

   MATTHEW 14:8

   A. STICK

   B. PLATTER

   C. BOWL

2. WHAT HAPPENED TO THE MEN THAT THREW SHADRACH, MESHACH, AND ABEDNEGO INTO THE FIERY FURNACE?

   DANIEL 3:22

   A. THEIR HAIR WAS SINGED.

   B. THE HEAT OF THE FIRE KILLED THEM.

   C. THEY GOT VERY WARM.

3. WHAT DOES JAMES SAY SHALL SAVE THE SICK?

   JAMES 5:15

   A. A DOCTOR

   B. GOING TO THE HOSPITAL

   C. A PRAYER OF FAITH

CONT'D NEXT PAGE...

WHAT WAS JOHN THE BAPTIST UNWORTHY TO UNTIE?

MARK 1:7

    A. JESUS' NECKTIE

    B. JESUS' CLOAK

    C. JESUS' SANDALS

WHY DID MARY AND JOSEPH GO TO BETHLEHEM?

LUKE 2:1-4

    A. FOR A VACATION

    B. TO REGISTER THEIR NAMES TO PAY TAXES

    C. TO VISIT ELIZABETH

WHAT HAPPENED TO THE WATERS OF MARAH WHEN MOSES THREW A TREE IN?

EXODUS 15:23-25

    A. THE TREE BLOCKED THE WATER.

    B. MADE THE WATER SWEET OR GOOD TO DRINK

    C. MADE A MESS

MULTIPLE CHOICE

CIRCLE THE CORRECT ANSWER.

1. WHAT WAS GIVEN TO PAUL TO KEEP HIM HUMBLE?

   2 CORINTHIANS 12:7

   A. A THORN IN THE FLESH

   B. BLINDNESS

   C. POVERTY

2. FOR WHAT DID ESAU SELL HIS BIRTHRIGHT?

   GENESIS 25:34

   A. HAMBURGER AND FRIES

   B. A BOWL OF STEW

   C. A NEW SUIT OF CLOTHES

3. WHAT DID JESUS SAY THE RICH MAN MUST SELL TO HAVE TREASURES IN HEAVEN?

   MATTHEW 19:21

   A. HIS HOUSE

   B. ALL HIS POSSESSIONS

   C. HIS BROTHER

CONT'D NEXT PAGE ...

. WHAT WAS FOUND IN BENJAMIN'S PACK ?

GENESIS 44:12

    A. A FROG

    B. HIS CLOTHES

    C. JOSEPH'S SILVER CUP

5. WHAT KIND OF TREE DID JESUS CONDEMN ?

MATTHEW 21:19

    A. AN APPLE TREE

    B. A FIG TREE

    C. A PLUM TREE

5. WHAT PARABLE TELLS OF THE SON THAT LEAVES HOME AND WASTES ALL HIS MONEY ?

LUKE 15:11-32

    A. THE STUBBORN SON

    B. THE FIRST SON

    C. THE PRODIGAL SON

FILL IN THE BLANKS

WORD LIST

DEEPLY	HOMES
LOOKING	OTHERS'
COMPLAINING	EACH
OPEN	LOVE

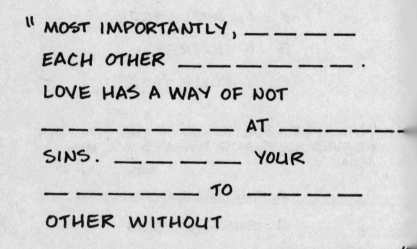

" MOST IMPORTANTLY, _ _ _ _
EACH OTHER _ _ _ _ _ _ _.
LOVE HAS A WAY OF NOT
_ _ _ _ _ _ _ AT _ _ _ _ _ _
SINS. _ _ _ _ YOUR
_ _ _ _ _ TO _ _ _ _
OTHER WITHOUT
_ _ _ _ _ _ _ _ _ _ _ !'

1 PETER 4:8-9

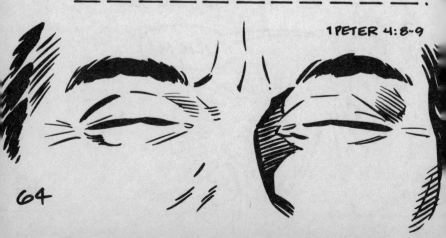

FILL IN THE BLANKS

WORD LIST

GIFT	GRACE
DIFFERENT	RESPONSIBLE
SERVANTS	YOU
GOD'S	EACH

" _ _ _ _ OF YOU RECEIVED A

SPIRITUAL _ _ _ _ . GOD HAS

SHOWN YOU HIS _ _ _ _ _

IN GIVING YOU _ _ _ _ _ _ _

GIFTS. AND _ _ _ ARE LIKE

_ _ _ _ _ _ _ _ WHO ARE

_ _ _ _ _ _ _ _ _ _ _

FOR USING _ _ _ _ GIFTS. "

1 PETER 4:10

READ 2 PETER 1:5-7. WHAT SHOULD YOU ADD TO EACH QUALITY BELOW?

LOOK ON THE FOLLOWING PAGE FOR YOUR ANSWERS.

FAITH

_____

GOODNESS

_____

KNOWLEDGE

_____

SELF-CONTROL

_____

ABILITY TO HOLD ON

_____

SERVICE TO GOD

_____

BROTHERLY KINDNESS

_____

THIS SCRIPTURE CONTINUES IN VERSES 8-9

" IF ALL THESE THINGS ARE IN YOU AND ARE GROWING, THEY WILL HELP YOU NEVER TO BE USELESS. THEY WILL HELP YOUR KNOWLEDGE OF OUR LORD JESUS CHRIST AND MAKE YOUR LIVES BETTER. BUT IF ANYONE DOES NOT HAVE THESE THINGS, HE CANNOT SEE CLEARLY. HE IS BLIND. HE HAS FORGOTTEN THAT HE WAS MADE CLEAN FROM HIS PAST SINS. "

WHAT A GREAT PROMISE !

KNOWLEDGE

ABILITY TO HOLD ON

LOVE

GOODNESS

SERVICE TO GOD

BROTHERLY KINDNESS

SELF - CONTROL

MATCH THE COLUMNS

WHO WAS WHOSE WIFE?

DRAW A LINE TO MATCH HUSBAND TO WIFE.

ABRAHAM

BOAZ

DAVID

KING XERXES

ELKANAH

HEROD

AQUILA

RUTH
RUTH 4:13

PRISCILLA
ACTS 18:2

HERODIAS
MARK 6:17

BATHSHEBA
2 SAMUEL 12:12

ESTHER
ESTHER 2:16-

HANNAH
1 SAMUEL 1:1-2

SARAH
GENESIS 17:15

68

TRUE / FALSE

JOSEPH WAS TWENTY-THREE YEARS OLD WHEN HIS BROTHERS SOLD HIM TO THE ISHMAELITES.

GENESIS 37:2   TRUE ____ FALSE ____

LAZARUS HAD BEEN DEAD FOR THREE DAYS WHEN JESUS CALLED HIM OUT OF HIS TOMB, RAISING HIM TO LIFE.

JOHN 11:39   TRUE ____ FALSE ____

MOSES AND ABRAHAM APPEARED WITH JESUS ON THE MOUNT OF TRANSFIGURATION.

MATTHEW 17:3   TRUE ____ FALSE ____

JESUS FED FOUR THOUSAND PEOPLE WITH A FEW LOAVES OF BREAD AND SOME FISH.

MATTHEW 15:29-38   TRUE ____ FALSE ____

69

MULTIPLE CHOICE

CIRCLE THE CORRECT ANSWER.

1. HE WANTED TO PUT HIS HAND IN JESUS' SIDE AFTER THE RESURRECTION. JOHN 20:24-2

    A. THOMAS

    B. JOHN

    C. PETER

2. JESUS CALLED HIM AWAY FROM HIS JOB AS A TAX COLLECTOR. MATTHEW 9:9

    A. PHILIP

    B. MATTHEW

    C. JAMES

3. JESUS HEALED HIS MOTHER-IN-LAW. MATTHEW 8:14-1

    A. JOHN

    B. JAMES

    C. PETER

CONT'D NEXT PAGE...

HE GAVE JESUS A KISS, BUT NOT OUT OF LOVE.

LUKE 22:47

    A. PONTIUS PILATE

    B. JUDAS ISCARIOT

    C. JOHN

HE BAPTIZED AN ETHIOPIAN HE MET ON THE ROAD.

ACTS 8:27-38

    A. PHILIP

    B. SIMON

    C. ANDREW

HE AND HIS BROTHER LEFT THEIR FATHER TO FOLLOW JESUS.

MATTHEW 4:18

    A. PETER

    B. THOMAS

    C. JUDAS

FINISH THE VERSE

HERE ARE SOME OF THE BEATITUDES.
FINISH THEM BY MATCHING THEM WITH
THE PHRASES ON THE FOLLOWING PAGE.

1. "BLESSED ARE THE POOR IN SPIRIT."

_____

2. "BLESSED ARE THOSE WHO MOURN."

_____

3. "BLESSED ARE THE MEEK."

_____

4. "BLESSED ARE THOSE WHO HUNGER AND
THIRST FOR RIGHTEOUSNESS."

_____

5. "BLESSED ARE THE MERCIFUL."

_____

6. "BLESSED ARE THE PEACEMAKERS."

_____

MATTHEW 5:1-10
(NEW INTERNATIONAL VERSION)

" THEY WILL BE COMFORTED."

" THEY WILL BE SHOWN MERCY."

" THEY WILL INHERIT THE EARTH."

" THEY WILL BE WITH GOD."

" THEY WILL BE CALLED SONS OF GOD."

" THEIRS IS THE KINGDOM OF HEAVEN."

" THEY WILL BE FILLED."

MATCH THE SAYING

MATCH THE SAYING BELOW WITH THE
PERSON WHO SAID IT FROM THE
FOLLOWING PAGE.

1. " YOUR FATHER AND I WERE VERY
WORRIED ABOUT YOU. WE HAVE BEEN
LOOKING FOR YOU. "
                              LUKE 2:48

_____

2. " I SINNED. I GAVE YOU AN
INNOCENT MAN TO BE KILLED. "
                              MATTHEW 27:4

_____

3. " AS FOR ME AND MY FAMILY, WE WILL
SERVE THE LORD. "
                              JOSHUA 24:14-15

_____

4. " NO! I WANT CAESAR TO HEAR MY
CASE! "
                              ACTS 25:10-11

_____

5. " I HAVE SINNED AGAINST THE
LORD. "
                              2 SAMUEL 12:13

_____

JUDAS

JESUS

PAUL

JOSEPH

DAVID

JOSHUA

MARY, HIS MOTHER

MOSES

JUDAS ISCARIOT

JOHN THE BAPTIST

FILL IN THE BLANKS

WORD LIST

ANSWER	MORNING
GOD	CRY
WAIT	YOU
NEED	VOICE

"LISTEN TO MY ___ ___ ___ FOR

HELP. MY KING AND MY ___ ___ ___

I PRAY TO ___ ___ ___. LORD,

EVERY ___ ___ ___ ___ ___ ___ ___ YOU

HEAR MY ___ ___ ___ ___ ___.

EVERY MORNING I TELL YOU

WHAT I ___ ___ ___ ___. AND

I ___ ___ ___ ___ FOR YOUR

___ ___ ___ ___ ___ ___."

PSALM 5:2-3

FILL IN THE BLANKS

WORD LIST

TIRED	WORK
HEAVY	SOULS
REST	EASY
LOADS	LEARN

" COME TO ME, ALL OF YOU WHO

ARE _ _ _ _ _ AND HAVE

HEAVY _ _ _ _ _. I WILL

GIVE YOU _ _ _ _. ACCEPT

MY _ _ _ _ AND _ _ _ _ _

FROM ME. I AM GENTLE AND

HUMBLE IN SPIRIT. AND YOU

WILL FIND REST FOR YOUR

_ _ _ _ _. THE WORK I

ASK YOU TO ACCEPT IS

_ _ _ _. THE LOAD I

GIVE YOU TO CARRY IS NOT

_ _ _ _ _. "

MATTHEW 11: 28-30

MULTIPLE CHOICE

CIRCLE THE CORRECT ANSWER.

1. HOW MANY TIMES DID JOSEPH AND
   MARY RUN FOR THEIR LIVES WITH JESUS

   MATTHEW 2:14-21

   A. ONCE

   B. TWICE

   C. THREE TIMES

2. HOW MANY DAYS DID GOD GIVE THE
   PEOPLE OF NINEVEH TO TURN FROM
   THEIR SIN OR THEY WOULD BE
   DESTROYED ?

   JONAH 3:4

   A. SEVEN DAYS

   B. FORTY DAYS

   C. TWENTY DAYS

3. HOW LONG DID IT GO ON WITHOUT
   RAINING AFTER ELIJAH PRAYED ?

   LUKE 4:25

   A. TWO AND A HALF DAYS

   B. THREE AND A HALF DAYS

   C. THREE AND A HALF YEARS

CONT'D NEXT PAGE...

HOW MANY PEOPLE DID KING
NEBUCHADNEZZAR SEE WALKING IN
THE FURNACE?

DANIEL 3:25

    A. THREE

    B. FOUR

    C. FIVE

HOW MANY BROTHERS DID JESUS
HAVE?

MARK 6:3

    A. NONE

    B. TWO

    C. FOUR

WHICH PLAGUE ON EGYPT INVOLVED
HAIL AND FIRE?

EXODUS 9:22-25

    A. THE THIRD

    B. THE FIFTH

    C. THE SEVENTH

MULTIPLE CHOICE

CIRCLE THE CORRECT ANSWER.

1. HOW OLD WAS JESUS WHEN HE WAS BAPTIZED AND STARTED HIS MINISTRY?

   LUKE 3:21-23

   A. ABOUT NINETEEN

   B. ABOUT TWENTY-FIVE

   C. ABOUT THIRTY

2. HOW LONG WAS MOSES ON THE MOUNTAIN TO RECEIVE THE TEN COMMANDMENTS?

   EXODUS 24:18

   A. OVERNIGHT

   B. FORTY DAYS

   C. FORTY DAYS AND NIGHTS

3. WHEN HE WAS PRAYING, HOW MANY TIMES DID JESUS WAKE HIS DISCIPLES IN THE GARDEN OF GETHSEMANE?

   MATTHEW 26:39-45

   A. ONCE

   B. TWICE

   C. THREE TIMES

CONT'D NEXT PAGE...

WHAT PIECE OF CLOTHING DID THE
SOLDIERS MAKE JESUS WEAR ?

JOHN 19:2-5

A. A WHITE ROBE

B. A PURPLE ROBE

C. A BLUE ROBE

WHAT WOMAN LED AN ARMY INTO
BATTLE ?

JUDGES 4:6-9

A. RUTH

B. DEBORAH

C. ESTHER

WHAT OTHER NAME WERE THE WISE
MEN CALLED ?

MATTHEW 2:1

A. SMART MEN

B. KINGS

C. MAGI

MATCH THE ANSWERS

MATCH THE ANSWERS ON THE FOLLOWING
PAGE TO THE QUESTIONS BELOW.

1. ON HIS THIRD MISSIONARY JOURNEY,
   WHERE WAS PAUL ARRESTED?

   _____   ACTS 21: 15-36

2. HOW MANY BASKETS OF BREAD WERE
   LEFT AFTER JESUS FED THE FOUR
   THOUSAND?   MATTHEW 15:34-3

   _____

3. WHO BROUGHT DORCAS, A DISCIPLE IN
   JOPPA, BACK TO LIFE?

   _____   ACTS 9: 39-41

4. WHO DID KING DAVID SEND TO THE
   FRONT LINE SO THAT HE WOULD BE
   KILLED IN BATTLE?   2 SAMUEL 11: 14-17

   _____

5. WHO WANTED JESUS' TOMB SEALED AND
   GUARDED SO NO ONE COULD STEAL THE
   BODY?   MATTHEW 27: 62-64

   _____

6. WHO THREATENED TO KILL ALL THE
   BELIEVERS OF JESUS?   ACTS 9:1

   _____

82

PAUL

PRIESTS

TWELVE BASKETS

ABSALOM

SAUL

JERUSALEM

SEVEN BASKETS

ROME

PHARISEES

PETER

URIAH

PONTIUS
PILATE

83

TRUE / FALSE

1. THE BOOK OF EXODUS RECORDS THAT JOSEPH DIED WHEN HE WAS ONE HUNDRED AND TEN YEARS OLD.

   GENESIS 50:26   TRUE ____ FALSE ____

2. MOSES WAS ABRAHAM'S FATHER.

   GENESIS 11:27   TRUE ____ FALSE ____

3. HAM, THE SON OF NOAH, HAD FOUR SONS.

   GENESIS 10:6   TRUE ____ FALSE ____

4. PONTIUS PILATE ORDERED THREE SOLDIERS TO GUARD JESUS' TOMB.

   MATTHEW 27:65   TRUE ____ FALSE ____

5. JONATHAN WAS SAMUEL'S SON.

TRUE / FALSE

JESUS WAS BORN IN JERUSALEM.

MATTHEW 2:12

TRUE ____ FALSE ____

THE THREE WISE MEN RETURNED TO KING HEROD WITH INFORMATION ABOUT JESUS.

MATTHEW 2:21

TRUE ____ FALSE ____

JESUS WAS CALLED A NAZARENE BECAUSE HE LIVED IN THE TOWN OF NAZARETH.

MATTHEW 2:23

TRUE ____ FALSE ____

PETER BETRAYED JESUS AS THE LORD HAD SAID HE WOULD.

JOHN 13:26

TRUE ____ FALSE ____

GOLIATH WAS AN ISRAELITE AND A FRIEND OF THE YOUNG DAVID.

1 SAMUEL 17:4

TRUE ____ FALSE ____

TRUE / FALSE

1. KING SAUL WANTED TO KILL DAVID
   BECAUSE OF HIS JEALOUSY.

   1 SAMUEL 19:1

   TRUE ___ FALSE ___

2. NOAH LIVED FOR NINE HUNDRED
   AND THIRTY-FIVE YEARS.

   GENESIS 9:29

   TRUE ___ FALSE ___

3. AT FIRST, JOSEPH FELT HE SHOULD
   DIVORCE MARY WHEN HE FOUND OUT
   SHE WAS PREGNANT.

   MATTHEW 1:19

   TRUE ___ FALSE ___

4. JESUS' FATHER, JOSEPH, WAS A
   SON OF DAVID.

   MATTHEW 1:20

   TRUE ___ FALSE ___

5. EMMANUEL MEANS "GOD WITH US"
   AND IS ANOTHER NAME FOR JESUS
   FROM THE OLD TESTAMENT.

   MATTHEW 1:23   TRUE ___ FALSE ___
   ISAIAH 7:14

MATCH THE SAYING

MATCH THE SAYING BELOW WITH THE
PERSON WHO SAID IT FROM THE
FOLLOWING PAGE.

" THIS PUNISHMENT IS MORE THAN
I CAN STAND !"
                                    GENESIS 4:13

_____

. " THERE IS ONLY ONE GOD. AND THERE
IS ONLY ONE WAY THAT PEOPLE CAN
REACH GOD. "
                                    1 TIMOTHY 1:1
                                              2:5

_____

. " BUT THE MOST HIGH DOES NOT LIVE IN
HOUSES THAT MEN BUILD WITH THEIR HANDS."
                                    ACTS 6:8
                                         7:48

_____

4. " SEE, TODAY I AM LETTING YOU CHOOSE A
BLESSING OR A CURSE. "
                                    DEUTERONOMY 5:1
                                              11:26

_____

5. " AS SURELY AS THE LORD LIVES, DAVID
WON'T BE PUT TO DEATH."
                                    1 SAMUEL 19:6

_____

TIMOTHY   NEHEMIAH

STEPHEN   MOSES

ISAIAH   CAIN

SAUL   JOB

JONATHAN   PAUL

" ... DAVID WON'T BE PUT TO DEATH! "

AT LEAST NOT TODAY...

88

TRUE / FALSE

LOT WAS THE SON OF ABRAHAM.

GENESIS 11:31

TRUE _____ FALSE _____

SAUL WAS NOT JONATHAN'S FATHER.
HE WAS DAVID'S FATHER.

1 SAMUEL 19:1

TRUE _____ FALSE _____

JONATHAN DID NOT LIKE DAVID AND
WANTED NOTHING TO DO WITH HIM.

1 SAMUEL 19:2

TRUE _____ FALSE _____

4. SHEM, NOAH'S SON, HAD AN OLDER
BROTHER NAMED JAPHETH.

GENESIS 10:21

TRUE _____ FALSE _____

5. MARY WAS PLEDGED, OR BETROTHED,
TO MARRY JOSEPH.

MATTHEW 1:18

TRUE _____ FALSE _____

MULTIPLE CHOICE
CIRCLE THE CORRECT ANSWER.

1. WHO WAS JACOB'S FIRST SON?

GENESIS 46:8

    A. ESAU

    B. REUBEN

    C. ISAAC

2. HOW MANY SONS DID TERAH HAVE?

GENESIS 11:26

    A. ONE

    B. TWO

    C. THREE

3. WHAT WAS NIMROD KNOWN AS?

GENESIS 10:9

    A. A GREAT WARRIOR

    B. A GREAT FARMER

    C. A GREAT HUNTER

CONT'D NEXT PAGE ...

WHAT WAS THE NAME OF SAMUEL'S FIRSTBORN SON?

1 SAMUEL 8:2

A. ABIJAH

B. JOEL

C. SAMUEL, JR.

HOW DID PETER ESCAPE FROM PRISON?

ACTS 12:7-10

A. HE DRILLED HIS WAY OUT.

B. HIS FRIENDS HID A FILE IN A CAKE.

C. AN ANGEL OF THE LORD GOT HIM OUT.

WHAT IS ONE OF THE FOUR LIVING CREATURES IN THE VISION OF HEAVEN?

REVELATION 4:7

A. A CAT

B. AN EAGLE

C. A BUDGIE

MULTIPLE CHOICE

CIRCLE THE CORRECT ANSWER.

1. WHO WROTE THE BOOK OF EPHESIANS IN THE NEW TESTAMENT ?

   EPHESIANS 1:1

   A. EPHESIA

   B. TIMOTHY

   C. PAUL

2. HOW MANY LOAVES OF BREAD AND FISH DID JESUS USE TO FEED THE FOUR THOUSAND ?

   MATTHEW 15:34

   A. THREE LOAVES OF BREAD AND SEVEN FISH

   B. SEVEN LOAVES OF BREAD AND A FEW FISH

   C. FOUR THOUSAND LOAVES OF BREAD AND FOUR THOUSAND FISH

3. THE SECOND PLAGUE ON EGYPT WAS..?

   EXODUS 8:1-15

   A. FROGS

   B. LOCUSTS

   C. FLIES

CONT'D NEXT PAGE...

• HOW DID SAUL KILL HIMSELF ?

                        1 SAMUEL 31:4

      A. HUNG HIMSELF

      B. FELL ON A SWORD

      C. ASKED HIS SERVANT TO DO IT

. HOW DID GOD GUARD THE WAY TO THE TREE OF LIFE?

                    GENESIS 3:24

      A. PUT GATES AROUND IT

      B. MADE IT INVISIBLE

      C. SENT CHERUBIMS AND A
           FLAMING SWORD

5. HOW DID GOD CREATE THE FIRST WOMAN ?

                    GENESIS 2:21-22

      A. OUT OF DUST

      B. OUT OF ADAM'S RIB

      C. OUT OF ADAM'S
           SHOULDER

FILL IN THE BLANKS

" ANYTHING I SAW AND
— — — — — —, I GOT FOR
— — — — — —. I DID NOT
— — — — — — — —
PLEASURE I — — — — — —.
I WAS — — — — — — — WITH
EVERYTHING I DID. AND THIS
PLEASURE WAS THE — — — — —
FOR ALL MY HARD — — — —."

ECCLESIASTES 2:10

FILL IN THE BLANKS

WORD LIST

WHAT	GAIN
JUST	I
WIND	HARD
CHASING	TIME

" BUT THEN __ LOOKED AT _____
I HAD DONE. I THOUGHT ABOUT
ALL THE _____ WORK.
SUDDENLY I REALIZED IT WAS
_____ A WASTE OF _____,
LIKE _____
THE _____ ! THERE IS
NOTHING TO _____ FROM
ANYTHING WE DO HERE ON
EARTH . "

ECCLESIASTES 2:11

FILL IN THE BLANKS

WORD LIST

FINAL	NOW
HONOR	OBEY
COMMANDS	MOST
PEOPLE	HEARD

" _ _ _ EVERYTHING HAS BEEN _ _ _ _ _ _. HERE IS MY _ _ _ _ _ ADVICE: _ _ _ _ _ _ GOD AND _ _ _ _ HIS _ _ _ _ _ _ _ _. THIS IS THE _ _ _ _ IMPORTANT THING _ _ _ _ _ _ CAN DO. "

ECCLESIASTES 12:13

96

FILL IN THE BLANKS

WORD LIST

EVERYTHING	PLAN
HIS	WORKS
LOVE	PEOPLE
GOD	KNOW

" WE _ _ _ _ THAT IN

_ _ _ _ _ _ _ _ _ _

GOD _ _ _ _ _ FOR THE

GOOD OF THOSE WHO _ _ _

HIM. THEY ARE THE

_ _ _ _ _ _ _ _ _

CALLED, BECAUSE THAT WAS

_ _ _ _ _ _ _ . "

ROMANS 8:28

97

MATCH THE SAYING

MATCH THE SAYING BELOW WITH THE
PERSON WHO SAID IT FROM THE
FOLLOWING PAGE.

1. "...I COME AGAINST YOU IN THE NAME OF
   THE LORD ALMIGHTY..."

   1 SAMUEL 17:45

   _____

2. "MANY WHO HAVE THE HIGHEST PLACE
   NOW WILL HAVE THE LOWEST PLACE
   IN THE FUTURE."

   MARK 10:29-31

   _____

3. "TO THOSE WHO ARE PURE, ALL
   THINGS ARE PURE."

   TITUS 1:1,15

   _____

4. "COME HERE. I'LL FEED YOUR BODY
   TO THE BIRDS OF THE AIR AND THE
   WILD ANIMALS."

   1 SAMUEL 17:23-44

   _____

5. "LOOK! I SEE HEAVEN OPEN. AND I SEE THE
   SON OF MAN STANDING AT GOD'S RIGHT SIDE"

   ACTS 7:56

   _____

JESUS   JEREMIAH

PAUL   SAUL

JOHN   GOD

GOLIATH   DAVID

JEROBOAM   STEPHEN

FILL IN THE BLANKS

WHY THE BOOK OF PROVERBS IS
IMPORTANT TO READ.

" THEY _____ WISDOM AND

SELF- _____ . THEY GIVE

UNDERSTANDING. THEY WILL

TEACH YOU HOW TO BE _____

AND SELF-CONTROLLED. THEY

WILL TEACH YOU WHAT IS

_____ AND FAIR AND

_____ . THEY GIVE THE

ABILITY TO _____ TO THOSE

WITH LITTLE KNOWLEDGE.

THEY GIVE KNOWLEDGE AND

GOOD _____ TO THE _____

PROVERBS 1:2-4

WORD LIST

CONTROL	THINK
HONEST	TEACH
SENSE	RIGHT
WISE	YOUNG

100

TRUE / FALSE

SAMSON LED THE NATION OF ISRAEL
FOR FIFTEEN YEARS.

JUDGES 16:31   TRUE ____ FALSE ____

WHEN THE SOLDIERS SAW THE ANGEL
AT THE TOMB OF JESUS, THEY BECAME
LIKE DEAD MEN.

MATTHEW 28:2-4   TRUE ____ FALSE ____

THIRD JOHN IS THE TWENTY-FIFTH
BOOK IN THE NEW TESTAMENT.

TRUE ____ FALSE ____

CONT'D NEXT PAGE...

4. CORNELIUS' OCCUPATION WAS TENT-
MAKING.

ACTS 10:1   TRUE ___ FALSE ___

5. WE BECOME CHILDREN OF GOD BY
PUTTING OUR FAITH IN JESUS CHRIST.

GALATIANS 3:26   TRUE ___ FALSE ___

6. JOHN THE BAPTIST CALLED HIMSELF
A VOICE.

MARK 1:2-3   TRUE ___ FALSE ___

MATCH THE ANSWERS

MATCH THE ANSWERS ON THE FOLLOWING PAGE TO THE QUESTIONS BELOW.

1. WHO ASKED, " WHAT CRIME HAS JESUS COMMITTED ? "

    _____ MARK 15: 14

2. WHO ASKED WHY JESUS ATE WITH THE TAX COLLECTORS AND SINNERS ?

    _____ MATTHEW 9:11

3. WHO SAID, " IT IS NOT THE HEALTHY WHO NEED A DOCTOR, BUT THE SICK " ?

    _____ MATTHEW 9:12

4. WHO SAID, "COME HERE, I'LL FEED YOUR BODY TO THE BIRDS OF THE AIR AND THE WILD ANIMALS " ?

    _____ 1 SAMUEL 17: 4-44

5. WHO ASKED, " AM I MY BROTHER'S KEEPER ? "

    _____ GENESIS 4:9

6. WHO ASKED, " WHY HAVEN'T YOU TAKEN CARE OF GOD'S TEMPLE ? "

    _____ NEHEMIAH 1:1 ; 13:11

MARK PHARISEES

ABEL JAMES

HOSEA CAIN

GOLIATH PILATE

ISAAC SAUL

NEHEMIAH JESUS

MULTIPLE CHOICE

CIRCLE THE CORRECT ANSWER.

. WHICH PROPHET MARRIED AN UNFAITHFUL WIFE NAMED GOMER?

    A. ISAIAH

    B. HOSEA

    C. JEREMIAH

        (ANSWER FOUND IN VERSE 2-3 OF ONE OF THE ABOVE CHOICES.)

2. WHO WAS ABRAHAM'S SECOND SON?   GENESIS 21:2-3

    A. ISAAC

    B. ISHMAEL

    C. CAIN

3. THE MAGI WERE ...

    A. SOLDIERS.   MATTHEW 2:11-12

    B. WISE MEN OR KINGS.

    C. SHEPHERDS.

CONT'D NEXT PAGE ...

4. WHAT DOES THE LORD PREPARE IN THE PRESENCE OF OUR ENEMIES?

PSALM 23:5

    A. OUR CLOTHES

    B. DINNER

    C. A TABLE

5. IN THE PARABLE OF THE SOWER, WHERE DID THE SEED FALL THAT WAS CHOKED?

MATTHEW 13:7

    A. ON ROCKY SOIL

    B. AMONG THORNS

    C. AMONG WEEDS

6. WHERE DID LAZARUS, MARTHA, AND MARY LIVE?

JOHN 11:1

    A. JERUSALEM

    B. BETHANY

    C. NAZARETH

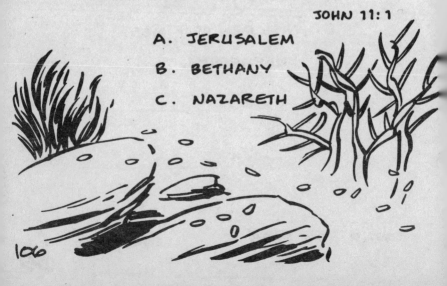

FILL IN THE BLANKS

WORD LIST

LOVED   KINGDOM

BELIEVES   CHILDREN

LIFE   LOVES

BORN   LIKE

. "FOR GOD _____ THE WORLD SO MUCH THAT HE GAVE HIS ONLY SON. GOD GAVE HIS SON SO THAT WHOEVER _____ IN HIM MAY NOT BE LOST BUT HAVE ETERNAL _____ ."

JOHN 3:16

2. "I TELL YOU THE TRUTH. UNLESS ONE IS _____ AGAIN, HE CAN— NOT BE IN GOD'S _____."

JOHN 3:3

3. " YOU ARE GOD'S _____ WHOM HE _____ . SO TRY TO BE _____ GOD."

EPHESIANS S:1

107

FILL IN THE BLANKS

WORD LIST

WORLD	TROUBLES
DEFEATED	HAPPY
HAPPEN	WISDOM
GENEROUS	GIVE

1. "MY BROTHERS, YOU WILL HAVE MANY
   _____ . BUT WHEN THESE THINGS
   _____ , YOU SHOULD BE VERY
   _____ ."
   JAMES 1:2

2. "I TOLD YOU THESE THINGS SO THAT
   YOU CAN HAVE PEACE IN ME. IN THIS
   _____ YOU WILL HAVE TROUBLE.
   BUT BE BRAVE! I HAVE _____
   THE WORLD!"
   JOHN 16:33

3. "IF ANY OF YOU NEEDS _____ , YOU
   SHOULD ASK GOD FOR IT. GOD IS
   _____ . HE ENJOYS GIVING TO ALL
   PEOPLE, SO HE WILL _____ YOU WISDOM.
   JAMES 1:5

MULTIPLE CHOICE

CIRCLE THE CORRECT ANSWER

. THE SHORTEST CHAPTER IN THE BIBLE IS ...

    A. PHILEMON 1.

    B. PSALM 117.

    C. TITUS 3.

2. WHO WAS CHOSEN TO REPLACE JUDAS ISCARIOT AFTER HE HANGED HIMSELF?

ACTS 1: 23-26

    A. JAMES

    B. MATTHIAS

    C. ANDREW

3. WHO WAS A "WILD DONKEY OF A MAN"?

GENESIS 16:11-12

    A. ISAAC

    B. JOHN

    C. ISHMAEL

CONT'D NEXT PAGE ...

109

4. WHAT EVANGELIST HAD FOUR DAUGHTERS
   WHO PROPHESIED ?

   ACTS 21:8-9

   A. ABRAHAM

   B. PHILIP

   C. ZACCHAEUS

5. AT WHAT HOUR OF THE DAY DID JESUS DIE?

   MARK 15:34-37

   A. THE THIRD HOUR

   B. THE NINTH HOUR

   C. THE SIXTH HOUR

6. HOW TALL WAS GOLIATH ?

   1 SAMUEL 17:4

   A. OVER EIGHT FEET

   B. OVER NINE FEET

   C. OVER TEN FEET

FILL IN THE BLANKS

EPHESIANS 6:13-17 IS ABOUT THE ARMOR OF GOD.

1. THE BELT OF _____ .

2. THE BREASTPLATE OF

_____.

3. FEET FITTED WITH _____ .

4. THE SHIELD OF _____ .

5. THE HELMET OF _____ .

6. THE SWORD OF THE _____ .

WORD LIST

TRUTH	RIGHTEOUSNESS
SPIRIT	FAITH
SALVATION	READINESS

WHO WAS HIS MOTHER?

MATCH SON TO MOTHER BY
DRAWING A LINE FROM ONE
NAME TO ANOTHER.

SOLOMON

RUTH
RUTH 4:13-17

SAMUEL

HAGAR
GENESIS 16:15

OBED

BATHSHEBA
2 SAMUEL 12:24

ISHMAEL

ADAH
GENESIS 36:4

ELIPHAZ

HANNAH
1 SAMUEL 1:20

TRUE / FALSE

. MATTHIAS REPLACED PETER AS AN
APOSTLE.

ACTS 1: 24-26

TRUE ____ FALSE ____

2. PHILIP BAPTIZED AN ETHIOPIAN
EUNUCH.

ACTS 8:38

TRUE ____ FALSE ____

3. THE DEATH OF THE FIRST BORN WAS
ONE OF THE PLAGUES OF EGYPT.

EXODUS 11: 4-6

TRUE ____ FALSE ____

4. JESUS SAID A PROPHET HAS HONOR
IN HIS OWN TOWN.

MATTHEW 13:55-58

TRUE ____ FALSE ____

CONT'D NEXT PAGE...

5. WHEN ABRAHAM DIED, GOD BLESSED HIS SON, ISAAC.

GENESIS 25:11

TRUE ____ FALSE ____

6. ABRAHAM WAS TESTED BY GOD.

GENESIS 22:1

TRUE ____ FALSE ____

7. THE QUEEN OF SHEBA CAME TO VISIT SOLOMON SO SHE COULD MARRY HIM.

1 KINGS 10:1-2

TRUE ____ FALSE ____

THE TEN COMMANDMENTS

NUMBER THEM SO THEY ARE IN THE RIGHT ORDER.

EXODUS 20: 3-17

_____ YOU SHALL NOT MAKE FOR YOURSELVES ANY IDOLS.

_____ YOU SHALL NOT LIE AGAINST YOUR NEIGHBOR.

_____ YOU MUST NOT MURDER ANYONE.

_____ YOU SHALL NOT STEAL.

_____ YOU MUST NOT BE GUILTY OF ADULTERY.

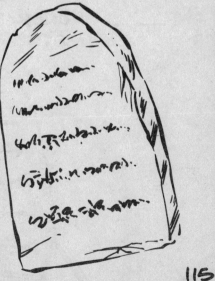

CONT'D NEXT PAGE...

115

_____ YOU SHALL NOT COVET
ANYTHING BELONGING TO
YOUR NEIGHBOR.

_____ YOU SHALL HAVE NO OTHER
GODS BEFORE ME.

_____ YOU MUST NOT USE THE NAME
OF THE LORD YOUR GOD
THOUGHTLESSLY.

_____ REMEMBER THE SABBATH
BY KEEPING IT HOLY.

_____ HONOR YOUR FATHER AND
MOTHER.

FILL IN THE BLANKS

WORD LIST

LOVE   SOUL

NEIGHBOR   HEART

LORD   MIND

GOD   YOURSELF

"_____ THE _____ YOUR
_____ WITH ALL YOUR _____
AND WITH ALL YOUR _____
AND WITH ALL YOUR _____."

MATTHEW 22:37

" LOVE YOUR _____ AS
YOU LOVE _____."

MATTHEW 22:39

FILL IN THE BLANKS

" MY CHILD, _____ TO YOUR _____ _____, AND DO NOT FORGET YOUR _____ _____ . "

" THEIR TEACHING WILL BEAUTIFY YOUR _____. IT WILL BE LIKE _____ IN YOUR HAIR OR A _____ AROUND YOUR NECK . "

PROVERBS 1: 8,9

MATCH THE ANSWERS

MATCH THE ANSWERS ON THE FOLLOWING
PAGE TO THE QUESTIONS BELOW.

1. WHERE WAS RUTH'S HOMELAND?

   _____ RUTH 1:1-7

2. WHO WAS THE THIRD SON OF ADAM?

   _____ GENESIS 5:3

3. WHERE WAS JACOB BURIED?

   _____ GENESIS 50:12-14

4. WHO SAID, "IF ANYONE IS NOT WITH
   ME, THEN HE IS AGAINST ME"?

   _____ MATTHEW 12:30

5. WHO WAS HOSEA'S FATHER?

   _____ HOSEA 1:1

6. IN THE GOSPEL OF JOHN, WHO DID
   JESUS WEEP FOR?

   _____ JOHN 11:31-35

ISAIAH   ESAU

SETH   MOAB

JESUS   CANAAN

JUDAH   PAUL

MARTHA   BEERI

LAZARUS   MARY

MATCH THE ANSWERS

MATCH THE ANSWERS ON THE FOLLOWING
PAGE TO THE QUESTIONS BELOW.

WHO WAS THE FIRST CHRISTIAN
MARTYR?

_____   ACTS 7:59-60

. WHAT TWELVE-YEAR-OLD GIRL WAS
BROUGHT BACK TO LIFE BY JESUS?

_____   LUKE 8:40-56

. WHO GAVE MOSES HIS NAME?

_____   EXODUS 2:10

4. WHO TOLD NOAH TO COME OUT OF
THE ARK?

_____   GENESIS 8:15-16

5. IN WHAT TOWN WAS JETHRO A
PRIEST?

_____   EXODUS 18:1

6. WHAT WAS THE NAME OF THE
CENTURION PAUL WAS HANDED OVER
TO?

_____   ACTS 27:1

PAUL

JAIRUS' DAUGHTER

HIS MOTHER

PHARAOH'S DAUGHTER

GOD

CORNELIUS

PETER'S DAUGHTER

JULIUS

HIS WIFE

MIDIAN

JERUSALEM

STEPHEN

MULTIPLE CHOICE

CIRCLE THE CORRECT ANSWER.

WHAT HAPPENED WHEN PHARAOH
WOULD NOT LET MOSES AND HIS
PEOPLE GO?

EXODUS 13:15

A. EVERY FIRSTBORN DIED.

B. EVERY SECONDBORN DIED.

C. THE RIVER DRIED UP.

2. TO WHAT DID PAUL COMPARE THE
COMING OF "THE DAY OF THE LORD"?

1 THESSALONIANS 5:2

A. A ROAR OF THUNDER

B. A FLASH OF LIGHTNING

C. A THIEF IN THE NIGHT

3. WHAT HAPPENED TO PETER WHEN JESUS
ASKED HIM TO WALK ON WATER?

MATTHEW 14: 29-31

A. HE DROWNED.

B. HE SANK FOR LACK OF FAITH.

C. AN ANGEL CARRIED HIM.

CONT'D NEXT PAGE ...

123

4. WHO WAS BLINDED BY JESUS ON THE WAY TO DAMASCUS?

ACTS 9:8

   A. PAUL

   B. SAUL

   C. PETER

5. WHO DID THE LORD CALL BY A VISION IN DAMASCUS?

ACTS 9:10

   A. ANANIAS

   B. PETER

   C. PAUL

6. WHAT DID THE ANGEL MEASURE THE CITY WITH?

REVELATION 21:16

   A. A MEASURING TAPE

   B. A STICK

   C. A SQUARE AS LONG AS WIDE AND HIGH

FILL IN THE BLANKS

" MY _____ , BELIEVE WHAT
I _____ AND _____
WHAT I _____ YOU.
_____ TO _____ . TRY
WITH ALL YOUR _____ TO
GAIN _____ . "

PROVERBS 2:1-2

125

FILL IN THE BLANKS

WORD LIST

HIM   KNOWLEDGE

LORD   INNOCENT

HONEST   PROTECTS

WISDOM   SHIELD

" ONLY THE _____ GIVES

_____ . _____ AND

UNDERSTANDING COME FROM

_____ . HE STORES UP WISDOM

FOR THOSE WHO ARE _____

LIKE A _____ HE

_____ THOSE WHO ARE

_____ . "

PROVERBS 2:6-7

MULTIPLE CHOICE

CIRCLE THE CORRECT ANSWER.

WHAT WAS THE FIRST TREE MENTIONED IN THE BIBLE?

GENESIS 2:9

    A. APPLE

    B. CEDAR

    C. TREE OF LIFE

HOW OLD WAS JOSHUA WHEN HE DIED?

JOSHUA 24:29

    A. ONE HUNDRED AND TEN

    B. ONE HUNDRED AND TWELVE

    C. SIXTY-SEVEN

3. WHO WAS MARY'S FATHER-IN-LAW?

MATTHEW 1:16

    A. DAVID

    B. ZECHARIAH

    C. JACOB

CONT'D NEXT PAGE...

4. WHOSE BONES WERE CARRIED FORTY
YEARS THROUGH THE DESERT?

JOSHUA 24:32

A. MOSES'

B. JOSEPH'S

C. ADAM'S

5. WHAT DID JAMES SAY MAN COULD
NOT TAME?

JAMES 3:8

A. A BEAR

B. A LION

C. THE TONGUE

6. HOW LONG WAS JONAH IN THE BELLY
OF THE FISH?

MATTHEW 12:40

A. THREE DAYS AND NIGHTS

B. SEVEN DAYS AND NIGHTS

C. THIRTY DAYS AND NIGHTS

H-H-HELP!

MULTIPLE CHOICE

CIRCLE THE CORRECT ANSWER.

. WHY DID MOSES BREAK THE TABLETS OF THE TEN COMMANDMENTS?

EXODUS 32:19

   A. THEY WERE TOO HEAVY.

   B. HE DROPPED THEM.

   C. HE WAS ANGRY AT THE ISRAELITES.

. WHAT WAS THE SIGN OF THE PROMISE BETWEEN GOD AND NOAH?

GENESIS 9:12-13

   A. A RAINBOW

   B. THE RAIN

   C. THE ARK

3. WHAT DOES THE NAME "EVE" MEAN?

GENESIS 3:20

   A. MOTHER OF EVENING

   B. MOTHER OF ALL LIVING

   C. BEGINNING OF NIGHT

CONT'D NEXT PAGE...

4. WHAT IS THE FOURTEENTH BOOK OF THE OLD TESTAMENT?

    A. SECOND CHRONICLES

    B. FIRST CHRONICLES

    C. SECOND KINGS

5. WHAT HAPPENED TO THE YOUTH THAT MADE FUN OF ELISHA'S BALDNESS?

    2 KINGS 2:23-24

    A. THEY WERE SENT TO THEIR ROOMS

    B. THEY WERE MAULED BY BEARS

    C. THEY HAD TO APOLOGIZE.

6. HOW OLD WAS JEHORAM WHEN HE BECAME KING OF JUDAH?

    2 CHRONICLES 21:5

    A. TWELVE

    B. THIRTY-TWO

    C. TWENTY-FIVE

UNSCRAMBLE THE VERSE

TO FIND OUT WHAT THE VERSE BELOW
SAYS, FILL IN THE BLANKS. ALL THE
VOWELS ARE THERE. ALL YOU NEED TO
DO IS ADD THE CONSONANTS.

" YM DCHLI , OD TNO TFEORG YM

GTNEIAHC. NTHE UOY IWLL

ELVI A GNLO MTEI. DNA RYUO

EIFL LILW EB SLSUUFCSCE. "

" __ __I__, _O _O_
_O__E_ __
_EA__I__.
__E_ _OU_I__
_I_E A _O__
_I_E. A___
_OU_ _I_E _I__
_E _U__E___U_."

PROVERBS 3:1-2

131

UNSCRAMBLE THE VERSE

TO FIND OUT WHAT THE VERSE BELOW
SAYS, FILL IN THE BLANKS. ALL THE
VOWELS ARE THERE. ALL YOU NEED TO
DO IS ADD THE CONSONANTS.

"TTSUR HET DLRO TWHI LAL
RUYO THARE. DTON DNDEPE
NO RYUO NOW DRENUNSINDTAG.
RREMMEBE ETH DLOR NI
EEVYRGNIHT UYO OD. DNA EH
LLWI EIGV YUO SSSCCEU."

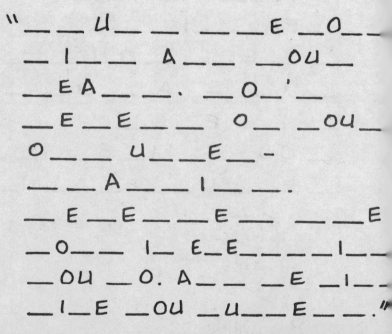

"__ U__ __ ___E _O__
_ I__ A__ __OU_
_E A__ __. _O_'_
_E _E __ _ O_ _OU_
O__ U__E__-
__A__I__.
_ E _E__ _E__ ___E
_O__ I_ E_E___ ___I__
_OU _O. A__ _E _I__
_I_E _OU _U__E__."

TRUE / FALSE

. MARY, JESUS' MOTHER, WAS NOT
AT THE CRUCIFIXION.

JOHN 19:25

TRUE ____ FALSE ____

. JESUS HAD NO BROTHERS OR
SISTERS.

MARK 6:3

TRUE ____ FALSE ____

. ISAIAH WAS AN APOSTLE.

2 CHRONICLES 32:20

TRUE ____ FALSE ____

CONT'D NEXT PAGE ...

133

4. JESUS WAS TWELVE YEARS OLD WHEN HE FIRST SPOKE AT THE TEMPLE.

LUKE 2:42-46

TRUE ___ FALSE ___

5. BARNABAS WAS A FOLLOWER OF JESUS.

ACTS 11:22-24

TRUE ___ FALSE ___

6. KING DAVID MOVED THE ARK OF THE COVENANT FROM THE HOUSE OF ABINADAB TO THE TABERNACLE.

2 SAMUEL 6:2-17

TRUE ___ FALSE ___

TRUE / FALSE

. SOLOMON WAS DAVID'S SON.

1 KINGS 2:1

TRUE _____ FALSE _____

2. DAVID KILLED SIX HUNDRED OF THE ARAMEAN CHARIOTEERS AND THIRTY THOUSAND OF THEIR FOOT SOLDIERS.

2 SAMUEL 10:18

TRUE _____ FALSE _____

3. ABRAHAM WAS TESTED BY GOD.

GENESIS 22:1

TRUE _____ FALSE _____

CONT'D NEXT PAGE ...

4. GOD DESTROYED SODOM AND GOMORRAH.

GENESIS 19:24

TRUE ____ FALSE ____

5. SIMON THE SORCERER BECAME A FOLLOWER OF JESUS CHRIST.

ACTS 8:13

TRUE ____ FALSE ____

6. ELISABETH, WIFE OF ZACHARIAS, WAS A DESCENDANT OF AARON.

LUKE 1:5

TRUE ____ FALSE ____

MATCH THE ANSWERS

MATCH THE ANSWERS ON THE FOLLOWING
PAGE TO THE QUESTIONS BELOW.

1. WHAT DID EZEKIEL EAT THAT WAS AS
   SWEET AS HONEY?

   EZEKIEL 3:3

   _____

2. WHO WAS TOLD IN A VISION ABOUT
   HIS SON'S BIRTH?

   LUKE 1: 11-13

   _____

3. IN WHAT PROVINCE DID JESUS MEET
   THE FISHERMEN?

   MATTHEW 4: 18-19

   _____

4. WHERE WAS JACOB BURIED?

   GENESIS 50: 12-14

   _____

5. WHO WAS SOLOMON'S MOTHER?

   1 KINGS 1:11

   _____

6. WHAT IS THE LAST WORD IN THE
   BIBLE?

   REVELATION 22: 21

   _____

ZACHARIAS   A HONEYCOMB

QUEEN OF SHEBA   JOSEPH

THE SCROLL   GALILEE

JERUSALEM   BATHSHEBA

JUDAH   EGYPT

THE END   AMEN

MATCH THE ANSWERS

MATCH THE ANSWERS ON THE FOLLOWING
PAGE TO THE QUESTIONS BELOW.

1. WHERE WAS JESUS BORN?

   LUKE 2:4-6

   _____

2. WHAT BABY WAS FOUND IN A BASKET
   IN A RIVER?

   EXODUS 2:3-10

   _____

3. WHAT WAS THE THIRD PLAGUE THE
   LORD BROUGHT ON PHARAOH?

   EXODUS 8:16-19

   _____

4. WHO WAS AARON'S SISTER?

   EXODUS 15:20

   _____

5. IN WHAT CITY WAS RAHAB AND THOSE
   IN HER HOUSE THE ONLY SURVIVORS?

   JOSHUA 6:17-25

   _____

6. IN WHAT MONTH DID THE ARK COME
   TO REST ON MOUNT ARARAT?

   GENESIS 8:4

   _____

EGYPT

NAZARETH

AARON

MOSES

BETHLEHEM

PLAGUE OF LICE

PLAGUE OF FROGS

ZIPPORAH

SEVENTH MONTH

MIRIAM

JERICHO

EIGHTH MONTH

MULTIPLE CHOICE

CIRCLE THE CORRECT ANSWER.

1. HOW MANY CHARIOTS AND HORSEMEN
    DID SOLOMON HAVE ?

    1 KINGS 10:26

    A . FOURTEEN HUNDRED CHARIOTS
        TWELVE THOUSAND HORSEMEN

    B . TWELVE THOUSAND CHARIOTS
        FOURTEEN THOUSAND HORSEMEN

    C . TWELVE THOUSAND CHARIOTS
        FOURTEEN HUNDRED HORSEMEN

2. WHERE DID ADAM AND EVE FIRST
    LIVE ?

    GENESIS 2:8

    A . BABYLON

    B . GARDEN OF EDEN

    C . ISRAEL

3. WHAT DID PAUL HAVE IN TROAS ?

    ACTS 16: 8-9

    A . A COLD

    B . A DREAM

    C . A VISION

CONT'D NEXT PAGE ...

4. THE NAME "ABRAHAM" MEANS...?

GENESIS 17:5

    A. FATHER OF NATIONS

    B. FATHER OF ISAAC

    C. FATHER OF ALL

5. HOW MANY DAYS DID WATER FLOOD THE EARTH?

GENESIS 7:24

    A. SEVEN DAYS

    B. THIRTY DAYS

    C. ONE HUNDRED AND FIFTY DAYS

6. HOW MANY PEOPLE WERE KILLED WHEN SAMSON DESTROYED THE TEMPLE OF DAGON?

JUDGES 16:22-30

    A. THREE THOUSAND

    B. THIRTY THOUSAND

    C. THREE HUNDRED THOUSAND

MULTIPLE CHOICE

CIRCLE THE CORRECT ANSWER.

WHAT HAPPENED TO PHARAOH'S ARMY WHEN THEY CHASED AFTER MOSES AND HIS PEOPLE?

EXODUS 14:26-28

A. THEY GOT SAND IN THEIR EYES.

B. THEY GOT TIRED OF THE CHASE.

C. THEY DROWNED IN THE RED SEA.

. WHAT DID ELIJAH CALL DOWN FROM HEAVEN?

1 KINGS 18:20-40

A. FIRE

B. RAIN

C. ANGELS

. HOW DID JUDAS IDENTIFY JESUS FOR THE SOLDIERS?

MATTHEW 26:48-49

A. BY POINTING HIM OUT

B. WITH A KISS

C. BY A HAND ON HIS SHOULDER

CONT'D NEXT PAGE ...

4. WHAT LESSON DID JESUS TEACH THE DISCIPLES BY WASHING THEIR FEET?

JOHN 13:5-16

    A. TO KEEP THEIR FEET CLEAN

    B. TO SERVE OTHERS HUMBLY

    C. ABOUT CEREMONIAL CLEANSING

5. WHAT DID GOD CREATE TO SEPARATE DAY FROM NIGHT?

GENESIS 1:14-19

    A. FIRE

    B. LIGHTS (STARS) IN THE SKY

    C. ELECTRIC LIGHTS

6. FINISH PAUL'S SENTENCE, "ALL PEOPLE HAVE SINNED AND..."

ROMANS 3:23

    A. ARE NOT GOOD ENOUGH FOR GOD'S GLORY

    B. SHOULD BE PUNISHED.

    C. NEED FORGIVENESS.

FINISH THE VERSE

TO FIND OUT WHAT THE VERSE BELOW
SAYS, FILL IN THE BLANKS. ALL THE
CONSONANTS ARE THERE. ALL YOU NEED
TO DO IS ADD THE VOWELS.

VOWELS : A E I O U

"D__N'T D_P_ND __N
Y___R __WN W_SD__M.
R__SP__CT TH_ L_RD
__ND R_F_S__ T_ D_
WR__NG. TH__N Y___R
B_DY W__LL B_
H___LTHY __ND Y___R
B__N__S W__LL B_
STR__NG."

PROVERBS 3:7-8

145

FINISH THE VERSE

TO FIND OUT WHAT THE VERSE BELOW
SAYS, FILL IN THE BLANKS. ALL THE
CONSONANTS ARE THERE. ALL YOU NEED
TO DO IS ADD THE VOWELS.

VOWELS: A E I O U

" MY CH_LD, D_ N_T
R_J_CT TH_ L_RD'S
D_SC_PL_N_. _ND
D_N'T B_ _NGRY WH_N
H_ C_RR_CTS Y___.
TH_ L_RD C_RR_CTS
TH_S_ H_ L_V_S,
J_ST _S _ F_TH_R
C_RR_CTS TH_ CH_LD
TH_T H_ L_V_S. "

PROVERBS 3:11-12

146

TRUE / FALSE

THE LORD CREATED THE GARDEN OF EDEN.

GENESIS 2:8

TRUE _____ FALSE _____

IT WAS IN THE CITY OF LUZ (OR BETHEL) WHERE JACOB HAD HIS DREAM OF THE LADDER.

GENESIS 28:10-19

TRUE _____ FALSE _____

LOT PLEADED WITH THE LORD TO SAVE SODOM.

GENESIS 18:16-33

TRUE _____ FALSE _____

CONT'D NEXT PAGE ...

4. ADAM PERSUADED EVE TO EAT FROM THE TREE OF THE KNOWLEDGE OF GOOD AND EVIL.

GENESIS 3:6

TRUE ____ FALSE ____

5. A RIVER FLOWED OUT OF THE GARDEN OF EDEN.

GENESIS 2:10

TRUE ____ FALSE ____

6. GOD CREATED ALL OTHER LIVING CREATURES BEFORE HE CREATED MAN.

GENESIS 1:20-

TRUE ____ FALSE ____

TRUE / FALSE

TROPHIMUS WAS THOUGHT TO HAVE BEEN
BROUGHT INTO THE TEMPLE WITH PAUL.

ACTS 21:26-29

TRUE _____ FALSE _____

. TROPHIMUS WAS AN EGYPTIAN.

ACTS 21:29

TRUE _____ FALSE _____

. JETHRO WAS MOSES' SON-IN-LAW.

EXODUS 18:12

TRUE _____ FALSE _____

CONT'D NEXT PAGE ...

4. AFTER JESUS HAD FASTED IN THE WILDERNESS, ANGELS MINISTERED TO HIM.

MATTHEW 4:11

TRUE _____ FALSE _____

5. THE LAKE OF FIRE IS THE SECOND DEATH IN THE BOOK OF REVELATION.

REVELATION 20:14

TRUE _____ FALSE _____

6. PAUL DID NOT VISIT ICONIUM TO PREACH THE GOSPEL.

ACTS 13:50- 14:1

TRUE _____ FALSE _____

MATCH THE ANSWERS

MATCH THE ANSWERS ON THE FOLLOWING
PAGE TO THE QUESTIONS BELOW.

WHO ROLLED BACK THE STONE FROM
JESUS' TOMB?

MATTHEW 28:2

_____

IN WHAT CITY THAT PAUL VISITED WAS
THERE A SIGN THAT READ, "TO A GOD
WHO IS NOT KNOWN"?

ACTS 17: 22-23

_____

WHO HAD A VISION OF A GREAT THRONE
SURROUNDED BY TWENTY-FOUR
ELDERS?

REVELATION 1:1; 4:4

_____

WHAT WAS URIAH'S OCCUPATION?

2 SAMUEL 11:15-17

_____

WHO WAS THE MOTHER OF KING JOASH?

2 CHRONICLES 24:1

_____

HOW MANY WIVES DID KING JOASH HAVE?

2 CHRONICLES 24:3

_____

TWO

THE DISCIPLES

THESSALONICA

PAUL

TENTMAKER

JEHOSHEBA

TWO HUNDRED

ATHENS

SOLDIER

JOHN

ZIBIAH

THE ANGEL OF
THE LORD

MATCH THE ANSWERS

MATCH THE ANSWERS ON THE FOLLOWING
PAGE TO THE QUESTIONS BELOW.

WHO SAID, "LOOK! I SEE HEAVEN OPEN AND
I SEE THE SON OF MAN STANDING AT GOD'S
RIGHT SIDE"?

ACTS 7:56-59

_____

WHO SANG, "GOD FILLS THE HUNGRY WITH
GOOD THINGS, BUT HE SENDS THE RICH
AWAY WITH NOTHING"?

LUKE 1:46-53

_____

WHO CALLED HIS FOLLOWERS "THE SALT
OF THE EARTH"?

MATTHEW 4:23; 5:13

_____

1. IN WHAT LAND WAS PAUL FORBIDDEN TO
PREACH BY THE HOLY SPIRIT?

ACTS 16:6

_____

5. WHAT KIND OF SNAKE BIT THE
APOSTLE PAUL?

ACTS 28:3

_____

6. HOW OLD WAS ISAAC WHEN JACOB AND
ESAU WERE BORN?

GENESIS 25:26

_____

PAUL   MARY

ELISABETH   JOHN

JESUS   STEPHEN

VIPER   ASIA

GARDENER   POISONOUS

TWENTY-SIX   SIXTY

OUCH...

MULTIPLE CHOICE
CIRCLE THE CORRECT ANSWER

. DANIEL WAS A ... ?

MATTHEW 24:15

    A. PROPHET.

    B. DISCIPLE.

    C. APOSTLE.

. WHO WAS MELCHIZEDEK ?

GENESIS 14:18
HEBREWS 5:10

    A. A PROPHET

    B. A PHARISEE

    C. A HIGH PRIEST

3. WHO IS BEELZEBUB ?

MATTHEW 12:24-27

    A. SATAN

    B. A PROPHET

    C. A KING

CONT'D NEXT PAGE ...

4. HOW MANY BOOKS ARE IN THE NEW TESTAMENT ?

    A. TWENTY

    B. TWENTY-SEVEN

    C. TWENTY-EIGHT

5. WHO WAS HOSEA'S FIRST SON ?

    HOSEA 1:3-4

    A. JEZREEL

    B. SIMON

    C. HOSEA, JR.

6. WHAT DID MOSES DO TO GET WATER OUT OF THE ROCK ?

    EXODUS 17:5-6

    A. HIT IT WITH A HAMMER

    B. STRUCK IT WITH HIS STAFF

    C. KICKED IT

MULTIPLE CHOICE

CIRCLE THE CORRECT ANSWER.

. WHEN THE ISRAELITES SPOKE OUT AGAINST GOD AND MOSES IN THE DESERT, WHAT DID GOD SEND THEM?

NUMBERS 21:4-6

    A. POISONOUS SNAKES

    B. QUAIL

    C. MANNA

. WHAT BROTHERS WERE GIVEN THE NAME, "SONS OF THUNDER"?

MARK 3:17

    A. JOHN AND JAMES

    B. CAIN AND ABEL

    C. PEREZ AND ZERAH

3. JESUS TAUGHT IN PARABLES; WHAT IS A PARABLE?

    A. A BOOK OF MANY STORIES

    B. A RIDDLE

    C. A WAY OF TEACHING BY COMPARING THINGS TO GET THE MEANING

CONT'D NEXT PAGE ...

4. THE NAME "ISAAC" MEANS...?

GENESIS 17:17
18:9-15

    A. ONE WHO LAUGHS.

    B. STRONG AND MIGHTY.

    C. GRATITUDE.

5. WHAT DOES THE NAME "ESAU" MEAN?

GENESIS 25:25

    A. BALD

    B. HAIRY

    C. SLIM

6. WHAT TEMPLE DID SAMSON TEAR DOWN WHEN HE REGAINED HIS STRENGTH?

JUDGES 16:22-30

    A. TEMPLE OF DAGON

    B. SYNAGOGUE

    C. JERUBBABEL'S TEMPLE

MATCH THE PARABLE

MATCH THE SCRIPTURE REFERENCE
ON THE FOLLOWING PAGE TO THE
PARABLE BELOW.

1. THE WISE AND FOOLISH BUILDERS.

   _____

2. THE MUSTARD SEED.

   _____

3. THE PEARL OF GREAT PRICE.

   _____

4. THE LOST SHEEP.

   _____

5. THE PRODIGAL SON.

   _____

6. THE WEDDING BANQUET.

   _____

7. THE GOOD SAMARITAN.

   _____

8. THE UNMERCIFUL SERVANT.

   _____

159

LUKE 15: 3-7

LUKE 7: 41-43

MATTHEW 7: 24-27

MATTHEW 22: 1-14

MATTHEW 18: 23-35

LUKE 15: 11-32

MARK 4: 30-32

LUKE 10: 30-37

LUKE 11: 5-8

LUKE 14: 7-11

MATTHEW 13: 45-46

LUKE 19: 11-27

FILL IN THE BLANKS

WORD LIST

WISDOM	SIGHT
OUT	REASON
LIFE	CHILD
NECKLACE	YOUR

" MY _____ , HOLD ON TO
_____ AND _____ .
DON'T LET THEM ____ OF
YOUR _____ . THEY WILL
GIVE YOU _____ . LIKE A
_____ THEY WILL
BEAUTIFY _____ LIFE. "

PROVERBS 3:21-22

FILL IN THE BLANKS

" THEN YOU WILL GO ON YOUR WAY IN _____. AND YOU WILL NOT GET _____. YOU WON'T _____ TO BE _____ WHEN YOU LIE _____. WHEN YOU ____ DOWN, YOUR _____ WILL BE _____.

PROVERBS 3: 23-24

ZZZZ Z ZZZ

FILL IN THE BLANKS

WORD LIST

KEEP	LORD
PEOPLE	GOOD
HELP	SAFE
TRAPPED	ABLE

" THE _____ WILL KEEP YOU

_____ . HE WILL _____ YOU

FROM BEING _____ .

WHENEVER YOU ARE _____ ,

DO _____ TO _____ WHO

NEED _____ . "

PROVERBS 3:26-27

BOING!

FILL IN THE BLANKS

WORD LIST

TEACH   GOOD

UNDERSTAND   TELLING

ATTENTION   TEACHING

FORGET   CHILDREN

" MY _____ , LISTEN TO YOUR
FATHER'S _____ . PAY
_____ SO YOU WILL
_____ . WHAT I AM
_____ YOU IS _____ .
DO NOT _____ WHAT I
_____ YOU. "

PROVERBS 4:1-2

MULTIPLE CHOICE

CIRCLE THE CORRECT ANSWER.

. RIGHT AFTER JESUS WAS BAPTIZED
A VOICE FROM HEAVEN SAID WHAT ?
MATTHEW 3:17

    A. "THIS IS MY SON AND I
       LOVE HIM. I AM VERY
       PLEASED WITH HIM."

    B. "THIS IS MY SON AND HE
       IS THE WAY TO HEAVEN."

    C. "THIS IS MY SON, FOLLOW
       HIM."

2. WHO ASKED JESUS WHETHER IT WAS
RIGHT TO PAY TAXES TO THE ROMANS ?
MATTHEW 22:15-21

    A. HIS PARENTS

    B. HIS DISCIPLES

    C. THE PHARISEES

3. HOW OLD WAS ENOCH WHEN THE LORD
TOOK HIM ?
GENESIS 5:23-24

    A. SIXTY-FIVE YEARS OLD

    B. THREE HUNDRED AND
       SIXTY-FIVE YEARS OLD

    C. SEVENTY YEARS OLD

165

ONT'D NEXT PAGE...

4. IN WHAT CITY WAS PAUL ALMOST WHIPPE
   FOR SPEAKING TO THE PEOPLE?

   ACTS 22:22-29

   A. ROME

   B. JERUSALEM

   C. MACEDONIA

5. HOW MANY YEARS DID GOD ADD TO
   KING HEZEKIAH'S LIFE?

   ISAIAH 38:5

   A. FIVE

   B. TEN

   C. FIFTEEN

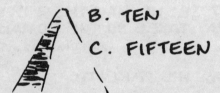

6. HOW MANY YEARS DID THE ISRAELITE
   LIVE IN EGYPT?

   EXODUS 12:40-41

   A. FOUR HUNDRED YEARS

   B. FOUR HUNDRED AND
                THIRTY YEAR.

   C. FIVE HUNDRED YEARS

MULTIPLE CHOICE

CIRCLE THE CORRECT ANSWER.

. WHERE DID MOSES GO AFTER KILLING
THE EGYPTIAN?

EXODUS 2:15

    A. HOME

    B. JUDAH

    C. MIDIAN

2. MOSES WAS WATCHING A FLOCK OF
SHEEP WHEN THE LORD CAME TO
HIM. WHOSE FLOCK WAS HE WATCHING?

EXODUS 3:1

    A. THE KING'S

    B. HIS FATHER'S

    C. JETHRO'S

3. IN WHAT MONTH DID THE ANGEL APPEAR
TO THE VIRGIN MARY?

LUKE 1:26-27

    A. THIRD MONTH

    B. SIXTH MONTH

    C. NINTH MONTH

CONT'D NEXT PAGE...

4. WHO MADE HIS WIFE PASS AS HIS SISTER ?

GENESIS 20:2

    A. MOSES

    B. ABRAHAM

    C. ISAAC

5. WHAT WAS THE POTTER'S FIELD KNOWN AS ?

MATTHEW 27:7-8

    A. FIELD OF BLOOD

    B. FIELD OF POTTERS

    C. FIELD OF DEATH

6. WHO TURNED HIS STAFF INTO A SNAKE ?

EXODUS 7:10

    A. MOSES

    B. AARON

    C. PAUL

MATCH THE ANSWERS

MATCH THE ANSWERS ON THE FOLLOWING
PAGE TO THE QUESTIONS BELOW.

1. WHO WAS EPHRAIM'S FATHER ?
   GENESIS 41:50-52

   _____

2. WHAT WAS HEZEKIAH'S
   OCCUPATION ?
   2 CHRONICLES 29:1

   _____

3. WHO WAS THE LAST PROPHET OF THE
   OLD TESTAMENT ?

   _____

4. ON WHAT MOUNTAIN DID MOSES
   RECEIVE THE TEN COMMANDMENTS?
   EXODUS 19:20-20:17

   _____

5. WHERE DID NOAH'S ARK COME
   TO REST ?
   GENESIS 8:4

   _____

6. WHO PLAYED A MADMAN TO ESCAPE
   FROM HIS ENEMIES ?
   1 SAMUEL 21:12-15

   _____

KING   DAVID

MALACHI   JOSEPH

HAGGAI   AARON

MOUNTAINS OF   PROPHET
         ARARAT

PAUL   MOUNT SINAI

ISAAC   MOUNT OF
              OLIVES

MATCH THE ANSWERS

MATCH THE ANSWERS ON THE FOLLOWING
PAGE TO THE QUESTIONS BELOW.

1. HOW MANY JARS OF WATER DID
   JESUS CHANGE TO WINE?

   JOHN 2: 1-10

   _____

2. WHAT OBJECT BROUGHT JOSEPH'S
   BROTHERS BACK TO EGYPT?

   GENESIS 44: 1-13

   _____

3. HOW MANY BOOKS OF THE BIBLE DID
   JESUS WRITE?

   _____

4. AT WHAT AGE DID LAMECH DIE?

   GENESIS 5: 31

   _____

   _____

5. WHO WAS LAMECH'S FATHER?

   GENESIS 5: 25

   _____

6. WHAT PROPHET WAS COMMANDED BY
   GOD TO GO TO NINEVEH?

   JONAH 1: 1-2

   _____

SEVEN JARS

A SILVER CUP

FOUR

NONE

SIXTY-SEVEN

JONAH

JOB

SIX JARS

METHUSELAH

A SILVER SPOON

AMOS

SEVEN HUNDRE
AND SEVENTY-SE

172

TRUE / FALSE

1. AT THE PASSOVER FEAST, JESUS SAID THAT ONE PERSON WOULD BETRAY HIM.

   MATTHEW 26:21

   TRUE _____ FALSE _____

2. JESUS RODE ON A HORSE TO JERUSALEM.

   MATTHEW 21:7

   TRUE _____ FALSE _____

3. JOHN WROTE THE BOOK OF REVELATION WHILE IN ROME.

   REVELATION 1:1-9

   TRUE _____ FALSE _____

CONT'D NEXT PAGE ...

4.   BARSABAS WAS AN APOSTLE.

ACTS 1: 23-26

TRUE _____ FALSE _____

5.   ABRAHAM LEFT EVERYTHING TO HIS
     SON ISAAC WHEN HE DIED.

GENESIS 25:5

TRUE _____ FALSE _____

6.   BECAUSE ESAU WANTED TO KILL
     JACOB, JACOB FLED TO HARAN.

GENESIS 27: 41-43

TRUE _____ FALSE _____

TRUE / FALSE

IT TOOK ELISHA JUST ONE TRY TO SET
FIRE TO HIS WATER-DRENCHED
SACRIFICE.

1 KINGS 18:36-38

TRUE _____ FALSE _____

. SOLOMON WAS MADE KING BEFORE
DAVID DIED.

1 KINGS 1:43-48

TRUE _____ FALSE _____

3. AARON DIED ON MOUNT HOR AFTER
MOSES GAVE HIS PRIESTLY CLOTHES TO HIS
SON.

NUMBERS 20:27-28

TRUE _____ FALSE _____

CONT'D NEXT PAGE ...

4. KING DARIUS HAD DANIEL TOSSED INTO THE LIONS' DEN.

DANIEL 6:6-16

TRUE _____ FALSE _____

5. NOAH'S SON JAPHETH WAS OLDER THAN HIS BROTHER SHEM.

GENESIS 10:21

TRUE _____ FALSE _____

6. JESUS WAS THIRTY-THREE YEARS OLD WHEN HE BEGAN HIS MINISTRY.

LUKE 3:23

TRUE _____ FALSE _____

WHO SAID ?

MATCH THE NAMES ON THE FOLLOWING
PAGE TO THE SAYINGS BELOW.

. " BUT IF A MAN IS ALREADY OLD, HOW
CAN HE BE BORN AGAIN ? "

JOHN 3: 4

_____

. " I AM NOT GUILTY OF THIS MAN'S
DEATH. YOU ARE THE ONES CAUSING
IT. "

MATTHEW 27: 24

_____

. " YOU WILL NOT DIE. "

GENESIS 3: 4

_____

4. " TEACHER , I WANT TO SEE. "

MARK 10: 46-57

_____

5. " HE MUST BECOME GREATER AND I
MUST BECOME LESS IMPORTANT. "

JOHN 3: 23-30

_____

6. " NO! YOU WILL NEVER WASH MY
FEET ! "

JOHN 13: 8

_____

SAMUEL   THE SERPENT

PONTIUS PILATE   THE THIEF

JOHN THE BAPTIST NICODEMUS

PETER   BARTIMAEUS

JOHN   DELILAH

MARK   REBEKAH

WHO SAID?

MATCH THE NAMES ON THE FOLLOWING PAGE TO THE SAYINGS BELOW.

. " I WILL GIVE HALF OF MY MONEY TO THE POOR. IF I HAVE CHEATED ANYONE, I WILL PAY THAT PERSON BACK FOUR TIMES MORE!"

LUKE 19: 8

_____

. . " A MAN HAS TOLD ME EVERYTHING I HAVE EVER DONE. COME SEE HIM. MAYBE HE IS THE CHRIST."

JOHN 4: 5-29

_____

3. " I HAVE SINNED AGAINST THE LORD."

2 SAMUEL 12: 13

_____

4. " I SINNED. I GAVE YOU AN INNOCENT MAN TO KILL."

MATTHEW 27: 3-4

_____

5. " COME FOLLOW ME. I WILL MAKE YOU FISHERMEN FOR ME."

MATTHEW 4: 18-19

_____

6. " BUT MAYBE YOU DON'T WANT TO SERVE THE LORD. YOU MUST CHOOSE FOR YOURSELVES TODAY. YOU MUST DECIDE WHOM YOU WILL SERVE."

JOSHUA 24: 2-15

_____

179

LUKE

DAVID

PETER

JESUS

JOSHUA

JUDAS
ISCARIOT

SAMUEL

MATTHEW

ZACCHAEUS

JOHN

ABRAHAM

THE SAMARITAN
WOMAN

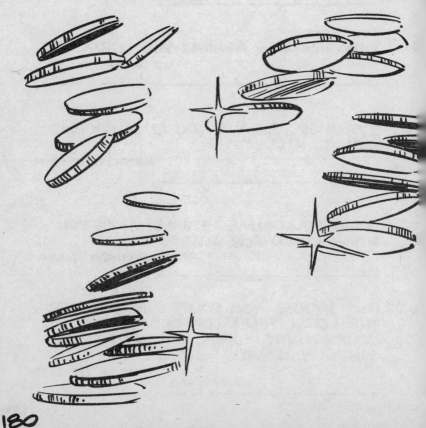

MULTIPLE CHOICE

CIRCLE THE CORRECT ANSWER.
WHO WAS JESUS SPEAKING TO
WHEN HE SAID THE FOLLOWING?

" HURRY, COME DOWN. I MUST STAY AT
YOUR HOUSE TODAY. "

LUKE 19:5

A. ANDREW

B. ZACHARIAS

C. ZACCHAEUS

.. " BEFORE THE ROOSTER CROWS TONIGHT,
YOU WILL SAY THREE TIMES THAT YOU
DON'T KNOW ME. "

LUKE 22:61

A. PETER

B. LUKE

C. JUDAS

3. " MARY HAS CHOSEN WHAT IS RIGHT, AND
IT WILL NEVER BE TAKEN AWAY FROM
HER. "

LUKE 10:41-42

A. LAZARUS

B. MARY MAGDALENE

C. MARTHA

CONT'D NEXT PAGE...

183

4. " THE ONLY POWER YOU HAVE OVER ME IS THE POWER GIVEN TO YOU BY GOD.'

JOHN 19:10-11

    A. THE SADDUCEES

    B. THE PHARISEES

    C. PONTIUS PILATE

5. " PUT YOUR FINGER HERE. LOOK AT MY HANDS. PUT YOUR HAND HERE IN MY SIDE. STOP DOUBTING AND BELIEVE."

JOHN 20:26-2⁻

    A. THOMAS

    B. PETER

    C. ANDREW

6. " DEAR WOMAN, HERE IS YOUR SON."

JOHN 19:26

    A. MARTHA

    B. MARY, JESUS' MOTHER

    C. MARY, WIFE OF CLEOPH

MULTIPLE CHOICE

CIRCLE THE CORRECT ANSWER.

WHO WAS THIS WOMAN?

THIS WOMAN POURED EXPENSIVE PERFUME ON JESUS' FEET AND WIPED IT OFF WITH HER HAIR.

JOHN 12:1-3

A. MARY MAGDALENE

B. MARY, MARTHA'S SISTER

C. MARY, JESUS' MOTHER

THIS WOMAN WAS THE ONE JESUS FIRST APPEARED TO AFTER HIS RESURRECTION.

MARK 16:9

A. MARY MAGDALENE

B. MARY, WIFE OF CLEOPHAS

C. MARY, MARTHA'S SISTER

THIS WOMAN RECEIVED, FROM JESUS, THE DISCIPLE JOHN TO 'BE HER SON.'

JOHN 19:25-27

A. MARY, WIFE OF CLEOPHAS

B. MARY, JESUS' MOTHER

C. MARY MAGDALENE

CONT'D NEXT PAGE ...

4. THIS WOMAN HAD SEVEN DEMONS DRIVEN OUT OF HER BY JESUS.

LUKE 8:2

A. MARY MAGDALENE

B. MARY, MARTHA'S SISTER

C. MARY, WIFE OF CLEOPHAS

5. THIS WOMAN WAS SCOLDED FOR NOT HELPING TO MAKE DINNER.

LUKE 10:39-40

A. MARY, WIFE OF CLEOPHAS

B. MARY, JESUS' MOTHER

C. MARY, MARTHA'S SISTER

6. THIS WOMAN'S BROTHER DIED, AND JESUS BROUGHT HIM BACK TO LIFE.

JOHN 11:19-43

A. MARY MAGDALENE

B. MARY, MARTHA'S SISTER

C. MARY, WIFE OF CLEOPHAS

FINISH THE VERSE

TO FIND OUT WHAT THE VERSE BELOW SAYS, FILL IN THE BLANKS. ALL THE CONSONANTS ARE THERE. ALL YOU NEED TO DO IS ADD THE VOWELS.

VOWELS : A E I O U

" MY CH_LD, L_ST_N _ND _CC_PT WH_T _ S_ Y. TH_N Y _ _ W_ LL H_V_ _ L_NG L_F_ . _ _M G_ _ D_ NG Y_ _ _N W_ SD_ M. _ND _ _M L_ _ D_ NG Y _ _ T_ D_ WH_T _S R_ GHT. "

PROVERBS 4:10-11

FINISH THE VERSE

TO FIND OUT WHAT THE VERSE BELOW
SAYS, FILL IN THE BLANKS. ALL THE
CONSONANTS ARE THERE. ALL YOU
NEED TO DO IS ADD THE VOWELS.

VOWELS: A E I O U

"MY CH_LD, P_Y
_TT_NT__N T_ MY
W_RDS. L_ST_N
CL__S_LY T_ WH_T
_ S_Y. D_N'T _V_R
F_RG_T MY W_RDS.
K__P TH_M D__P
W_TH_N Y__R
H__RT."

PROVERBS 4:20-21

UNSCRAMBLE THE VERSE

TO FIND OUT WHAT THE VERSE BELOW SAYS, FILL IN THE BLANKS. ALL THE VOWELS ARE THERE. ALL YOU NEED TO DO IS ADD THE CONSONANTS.

" TEEHS DWROS REA ETH CREEST OT FLEI OFR SEOHT OHW NFDI EMHT. EYHT GNRIB HETHAL TO HET LHWEO DBYO. EB RVEY FCAULRE TBUOA WAHT UYO HTIKN ORYU TGSHHTUO RNU UORY FEIL."

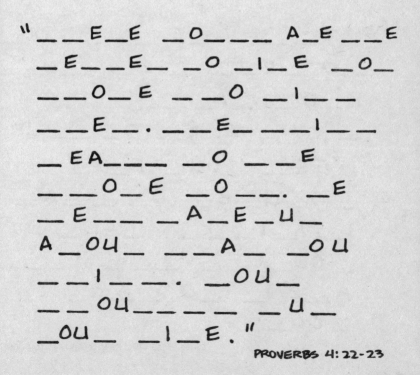

" _ _ E _ E _ O _ _ _ A _ E _ _ E
_ E _ _ E _ _ O _ I _ E _ O _
_ _ O _ E _ _ O _ I _ _
_ _ E _ . _ _ E _ _ _ I _ _
_ E A _ _ _ _ O _ _ E
_ _ O _ E _ O _ _ . _ E
_ E _ _ _ A _ E _ U _
A _ O U _ _ _ A _ _ O U
_ _ I _ _ . _ O U _
_ _ O U _ _ _ _ _ _ U _
_ O U _ _ I _ E . "

PROVERBS 4: 22-23

187

UNSCRAMBLE THE VERSE

TO FIND OUT WHAT THE VERSE BELOW
SAYS, FILL IN THE BLANKS. ALL THE
VOWELS ARE THERE. ALL YOU NEED
TO DO IS ADD THE CONSONANTS.

" NTOD SEU RYUO HMTOU OT LTEL

SLEI. NDOT VREE AYS GHTSIN TTH.

EAR TNO RUTE. KEPE YORU YEES

UCESDOF NO WTHA SI ITRHG. EEPK

LKNOGOI RGHTTSIA HDEAA OT AWTI.

SI DGOO. "

" _O_'_ U_E _OU_ _OU_
_O _E__ __IE_. _O_'_
E_E_ __A_ __I___
__A_ A_E _O_ __UE.
_EE_ _OU_ E_E_
_O_U_E_ O_ ___A_
I_ _I___. _EE_
_OO_'__ ___AI___
A__EA_ _O __A_ I_
_OO_ . "

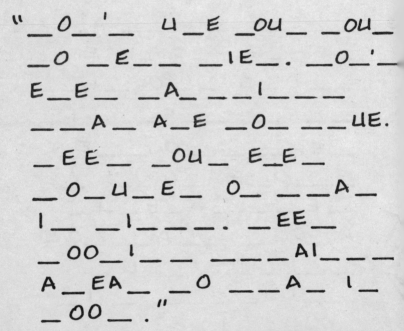

PROVERBS 4:24-25

188

TRUE / FALSE

1. JONAH TOLD THE PEOPLE OF NINEVEH THAT THEIR CITY WOULD BE DESTROYED IN FORTY DAYS.

JONAH 3:4

TRUE _____ FALSE _____

2. GOLIATH CHALLENGED THE ISRAELITES THREE TIMES A DAY FOR FORTY DAYS.

1 SAMUEL 17:16

TRUE _____ FALSE _____

3. ABRAHAM'S SERVANT WENT ALL THE WAY TO MESOPOTAMIA TO FIND A WIFE FOR ISAAC.

GENESIS 24:2-10

TRUE _____ FALSE _____

CONT'D NEXT PAGE...

189

4. DANIEL AND HIS FRIENDS ATE NOTHING BUT MEAT AND VEGETABLES FOR TEN DAYS.

DANIEL 1:12

TRUE _____ FALSE _____

5. WHEN THE RESIDENTS OF NINEVEH REPENTED, THEY PUT SACKCLOTH ON ALL THEIR ANIMALS.

JONAH 3:8

TRUE _____ FALSE _____

6. MORDECAI ACTED LIKE ESTHER'S FATHER, BUT HE WAS REALLY HER COUSIN.

ESTHER 2:7

TRUE _____ FALSE _____

TRUE / FALSE

. LAZARUS HAD BEEN IN THE TOMB FOR THREE DAYS BEFORE JESUS CALLED HIM OUT.

JOHN 11:39

TRUE _____ FALSE _____

. JOSEPH WAS TWENTY-THREE YEARS OLD WHEN HIS BROTHERS SOLD HIM TO THE ISHMAELITES.

GENESIS 37:2

TRUE _____ FALSE _____

. BEFORE HIS MINISTRY, JESUS WAS A CARPENTER.

MARK 6:3

TRUE _____ FALSE _____

CONT'D NEXT PAGE ...

191

4. AFTER MOSES WAS GIVEN THE TEN COMMANDMENTS, HE WORE A VEIL OVER HIS GLOWING FACE.

EXODUS 34:33-35

TRUE_____ FALSE _____

5. THE LEVITES HAD TO RETIRE AT THE AGE OF SIXTY-FIVE.

NUMBERS 8:23-2

TRUE _____ FALSE _____

6. AFTER SAUL KILLED HIMSELF, THE PHILISTINES CUT OFF HIS HEAD AND HUNG IT IN A TEMPLE.

1 CHRONICLES 10:8-10

TRUE _____ FALSE _____

MULTIPLE CHOICE

CIRCLE THE CORRECT ANSWER.

1. WHAT WERE THE LAST WORDS JESUS SPOKE ON THE CROSS?

   JOHN 19:30

   A. "I AM THIRSTY."

   B. "FATHER, FORGIVE THEM."

   C. "IT IS FINISHED."

2. WHEN JOSEPH BURIED JESUS, WHO WAS WITH HIM?

   JOHN 19:38-39

   A. JOHN

   B. NICODEMUS

   C. JESUS' MOTHER

3. JESUS WAS KNOWN AS A...?

   MATTHEW 2:23

   A. NAZARENE

   B. ISRAELITE

   C. ROMAN

CONT'D NEXT PAGE...

193

4. WHAT DOES "EMMANUEL" MEAN ?

MATTHEW 1:23

    A. JESUS WITH US

    B. GOD WITH US

    C. FATHER WITH US

5. WHO STAYED WITH NAOMI RATHER THAN RETURN TO HER OWN PEOPLE ?

RUTH 1:16-19

    A. ORPAH

    B. MOAB

    C. RUTH

6. WHERE WILL YOU FIND THE BOOK OF GALATIANS ?

    A. THE OLD TESTAMENT

    B. THE NEW TESTAMENT

    C. THE DICTIONARY

MULTIPLE CHOICE

CIRCLE THE CORRECT ANSWER

1. WHO WAS ON TRIAL AT THE SAME TIME AS JESUS ?

    MATTHEW 27:15-18

    A. BARABBAS

    B. JUDA

    C. PHARISEES

2. WHERE DID THE DEMONS BEG JESUS TO ALLOW THEM TO GO AFTER THEY WERE CAST OUT OF THE TWO MEN ?

    MATTHEW 8:32

    A. A HERD OF SHEEP

    B. A HERD OF COWS

    C. A HERD OF PIGS

3. AFTER JESUS HEALED THE TWO BLIND MEN, HE TOLD THEM TO ...?

    MATTHEW 9:30

    A. BE SILENT ABOUT IT.

    B. GO TELL THE PHARISEES.

    C. GO WASH THEIR FACES.

CONT'D NEXT PAGE ...

195

4. WHO DIVIDED THE JORDAN RIVER
   WITH HIS CLOAK?

   2 KINGS 2:8

   A. JOSHUA

   B. ELIJAH

   C. DANIEL

5. WHO BUILT A CALF OF GOLD TO MAKE
   THE ISRAELITES HAPPY?

   EXODUS 32:1-4

   A. MOSES

   B. AARON

   C. JONAH

6. WHAT WAS ANDREW'S OCCUPATION
   BEFORE HE WAS CALLED BY JESUS?

   MATTHEW 4:18

   A. A CARPENTER

   B. A TAX COLLECTOR

   C. A FISHERMAN

196

WHO WAS HIS MOTHER?

MATCH MOTHER TO SON BY
DRAWING A LINE FROM ONE
NAME TO ANOTHER.

HAGGITH   JOSEPH
    1 KINGS 1:5

RACHEL   AHAZIAH
    GENESIS 30: 22-24

AHINOAM   ADONIJAH
    1 SAMUEL 14: 49-50

ATHALIAH   JUDAH
    2 KINGS 8:26

LEAH   JONATHAN
    GENESIS 29:32-35

GOO-- GOO-- GOOO...

197

MULTIPLE CHOICE
CIRCLE THE CORRECT ANSWER.

1. HOW MANY YEARS DID SAMSON JUDGE ISRAEL?

   JUDGES 16:31

   A. FIVE YEARS

   B. TWENTY YEARS

   C. FIFTEEN YEARS

2. WHAT HAPPENED TO THE SOLDIERS WHEN THEY SAW THE ANGEL AT THE TOMB?

   MATTHEW 28:2-4

   A. THEY RAN.

   B. THEY SANG.

   C. THEY BECAME LIKE DEAD MEN.

3. WHAT IS THE TWENTY-FIFTH BOOK OF THE NEW TESTAMENT?

   A. 1 JOHN

   B. REVELATION

   C. 3 JOHN

CONT'D NEXT PAGE ...

4. WHAT WAS CORNELIUS' OCCUPATION?

ACTS 10:1

    A. A COOK

    B. A TENTMAKER

    C. A CENTURION

5. PAUL SAID, "YOU ARE ALL THE CHILDREN OF GOD BY..."

GALATIANS 3:26

    A. "GETTING BAPTIZED."

    B. "FAITH IN JESUS CHRIST."

    C. "GOING TO CHURCH."

6. WHAT MAN CALLED HIMSELF A VOICE CRYING OUT IN THE WILDERNESS?

MARK 1:2-8

    A. ELIJAH

    B. JOHN THE BAPTIST

    C. JOHN

Answer Pages

USING THE WORD LIST BELOW, FILL IN
THE BLANKS TO COMPLETE THE VERSES.

"__HAPPY__ IS THE PERSON
WHO DOESN'T __LISTEN__
TO THE WICKED. HE DOESN'T
GO WHERE __SINNERS__
GO. HE DOESN'T DO WHAT
__BAD__ PEOPLE DO. HE LOVES
THE __LORD'S__ TEACHINGS.
HE THINKS ABOUT THOSE
__TEACHINGS__
__DAY__ AND __NIGHT__."

PSALM 1: 1-2

WORD LIST	
TEACHINGS	LISTEN
BAD	DAY
NIGHT	SINNERS
HAPPY	LORD'S

1

... CONT'D FROM PREVIOUS PAGE .

4. HOW MANY DISCIPLES HAD THE NAME
OF JAMES?

MATTHEW 10:2-3

  (A) TWO
  B. FOUR
  C. SEVEN

5. WHAT DOES THE HEBREW WORD, "ABBA,"
MEAN?

ROMANS 8:6

  A. HELLO
  (B) DADDY
  C. MOMMY

6. WHO DID JESUS SAY THE SABBATH
WAS MADE FOR?

MARK 2:27

  A. GOD
  B. UNBELIEVERS
  (C) MAN

5

HOW MUCH OF THE BIBLE DO YOU KNOW?

MATCH THE ANSWERS ON THE FOLLOWING
PAGE TO THE QUESTIONS BELOW.

1. WHO SAID, "I AM WHO I AM"?
__GOD__

EXODUS 3:14

2. WHAT DID GOD CREATE ON THE FIRST DAY?
__LIGHT__

GENESIS 1:1-5

3. WHO BUILT THE ARK?
__NOAH__

GENESIS 6:13-14

4. HOW MANY SONS DID NOAH HAVE?
__THREE__

5. WHAT WERE THE NAMES OF NOAH'S SONS?
__HAM__ __SHEM__ __JAPHETH__

6. WHO SAID, " AM I SUPPOSED TO TAKE
CARE OF MY BROTHER"?
__CAIN__

GENESIS 4:9

2

MATCH THE ANSWERS
MATCH THE ANSWERS ON THE FOLLOWING
PAGE TO THE QUESTIONS BELOW.

1. WHO ASKED GOD TO SPARE SODOM?
__ABRAHAM__

GENESIS 18:23-33

2. WHO WROTE FIRST AND SECOND CORINTHIANS?
__PAUL__

1 CORL.1:1 , 2 COR.1:1

3. WHO DID JESUS SAY WILL INHERIT THE
EARTH?
__THE MEEK__

MATTHEW 5:5

4. WHAT IS THE NAME GIVEN TO JESUS
THAT MEANS "GOD IS WITH US"?
__EMMANUEL__

MATTHEW 1:23

5. WHAT WILL GOD GIVE US PLENTY OF IF
WE ASK HIM?
__WISDOM__

JAMES 1:5

6. WHERE IN EGYPT DID JOSEPH'S
FAMILY LIVE?
__GOSHEN__

GENESIS 47:6

6

MULTIPLE CHOICE
CIRCLE THE CORRECT ANSWER

1. WHOSE LIFE WAS SAVED BY BEING LOWERED
OVER A WALL IN A BASKET?

ACTS 9:25

  A JOHN'S
  B THE CRIPPLED MAN
  (C) SAUL'S

2. DAVID SAID THAT GOD MADE MAN A
LITTLE LOWER THAN WHAT?

PSALM 8:5

  A STARS
  (B) ANGELS
  C ANIMALS

3. WHERE WAS MOSES STANDING WHEN
GOD TOLD HIM TO TAKE OFF HIS SHOES?

EXODUS 3:5

  A ON A MOUNTAIN
  (B) ON HOLY GROUND
  C ON A BEACH

CONT'D ON NEXT PAGE ...

4

MULTIPLE CHOICE
CIRCLE THE CORRECT ANSWER.

1. WHAT WAS SARAH'S NAME BEFORE
GOD CHANGED IT?

GENESIS 17:

  A. SALLY
  B. HAGAR
  (C) SARAI

2. WHO DID PAUL CALL HIS OWN SON?

1 TIMOTHY 1:2

  A. PETER
  (B) TIMOTHY
  C. JOHN

3. WHO PREACHED ON THE DAY OF
PENTECOST?

ACTS 2:14

  A. JOHN
  B. PAUL
  (C) PETER

8

...cont'd from previous page.

4. WHO DID JACOB WEAR TO TRICK HIS FATHER? Genesis 27:15-24

A. SHEEPSKIN
B. BEARSKIN
C. GOATSKIN

5. HOW MANY PLAGUES DID GOD BRING ON EGYPT? Exodus 7-11

A. SEVEN
B. TEN
C. TWELVE

6. WHAT WAS THE NAME OF THE WELL THAT THE SAMARITAN WOMAN DREW WATER FROM? John 4:6-7

A. SAMARIA WELL
B. JOSEPH'S WELL
C. JACOB'S WELL

9

FILL IN THE BLANKS

WORD LIST	
LIFE	RESURRECTION
FOOL	WICKED
LORD	SHEPHERD
EVERYTHING	NEED

1. IN JOHN 11:25, JESUS SAID, "I AM THE **RESURRECTION** AND THE **LIFE**."

2. IN PSALM 14:1, IT SAYS, "A **WICKED FOOL** SAYS TO HIMSELF, 'THERE IS NO GOD'."

3. IN PSALM 23:1, IT SAYS, "THE **LORD** IS MY **SHEPHERD**. I HAVE **EVERYTHING** I **NEED**."

10

FILL IN THE BLANKS

WORD LIST		
LIGHT	CREATED	FEMALE
SAVES	IMAGE	
PROTECTS	AFRAID	
WAY	TRUTH	
LIFE	MALE	

1. IN PSALM 27:1, IT SAYS, "THE LORD IS MY **LIGHT**, AND THE ONE WHO **SAVES** ME. I FEAR NO ONE. THE LORD **PROTECTS** MY LIFE. I AM **AFRAID** OF NO ONE."

2. IN JOHN 14:6, JESUS SAID, "I AM THE **WAY**. I AM THE **TRUTH** AND THE **LIFE**."

3. IN GENESIS 1:27, IT SAYS, "SO GOD **CREATED** HUMAN BEINGS IN HIS **IMAGE**. IN THE IMAGE OF GOD HE CREATED THEM. HE CREATED THEM **MALE** AND **FEMALE**."

11

MATCH THE ANSWERS

MATCH THE ANSWERS ON THE FOLLOWING PAGE TO THE QUESTIONS BELOW.

1. WHO WAS ISHMAEL'S MOTHER? Genesis 16:15
   HAGAR

2. WHO WAS THE FATHER OF MANY NATIONS? Genesis 17:1-8
   ABRAHAM

3. WHO WAS THE BROTHER OF MARTHA AND MARY? John 11:1-2
   LAZARUS

4. WHAT IS THE ROOT OF ALL EVIL? 1 Timothy 6:10
   LOVE OF MONEY

5. WHAT IS THE JEWISH DAY OF REST CALLED? Exodus 20:10
   SABBATH

6. IN WHAT AREA IS BETHLEHEM LOCATED? Matthew 2:1
   JUDEA

12

MULTIPLE CHOICE

CIRCLE THE CORRECT ANSWER.

1. WHAT WAS THE NAME OF ABRAHAM'S PROMISED SON? Genesis 21:3

A. ISHMAEL
B. RONALD
C. ISAAC

2. WHAT WAS THE NAME OF JACOB'S YOUNGEST SON? Genesis 35:18

A. JOSEPH
B. JUDAH
C. BENJAMIN

3. WHO DID AQUILA AND PRISCILLA MEET IN CORINTH? Acts 18:1-2

A. JOHN
B. PAUL
C. PETER

cont'd on next page...

14

...cont'd from previous page.

4. WHAT DID KING BELSHAZZAR SEE ON THE? Daniel 5:1-9

A. FINGER PRINTS
B. A HAND WRITING
C. A BUG

5. WHAT DID GOD MAKE GROW OVER JONAH TO GIVE HIM SHADE? Jonah 4:6

A. A HOUSE
B. A TREE
C. A VINE

6. WHERE DID KING SOLOMON FIND CEDAR TREES FOR THE TEMPLE? 1 Kings 5:6

A. A LUMBER STORE
B. HIS BACK YARD
C. LEBANON

15

MULTIPLE CHOICE

CIRCLE THE CORRECT ANSWER.

HOW MANY BOOKS ARE THERE IN THE BIBLE?

A. SIXTY-EIGHT
B. SIXTY-SIX
C. THIRTY-FOUR

WHAT COMMANDMENT SAYS, "YOU MUST NOT MURDER ANYONE"? Exodus 20:13

A. TWELFTH
B. SIXTH
C. SEVENTH

HOW MANY BOOKS ARE IN THE NEW TESTAMENT?

A. TWENTY-SIX
B. TWENTY-EIGHT
C. TWENTY-SEVEN

cont'd on next page...

16

...cont'd from previous page.

4. HOW MANY FRIENDS CAME TO SPEAK WITH JOB? Job 2:11

A. ONE
B. THREE
C. THIRTY-SIX

5. ON WHICH DAY DID GOD CREATE THE SUN, MOON, AND STARS? Genesis 1:14-19

A. SECOND
B. FOURTH
C. SIXTH

6. HOW MANY TIMES DID JESUS ASK PETER IF HE LOVED HIM? John 21:15-17

A. ONE
B. THREE
C. FIVE

17

FILL IN THE BLANKS

WORD LIST		
PATIENT	TRUST	ANGRY
JEALOUS	RUDE	HOPES
TRUTH	SELFISH	WRONGS
BRAG	STRONG	HAPPY
PROUD	KIND	

"LOVE IS **PATIENT** AND **KIND**. LOVE IS NOT **JEALOUS**. IT DOES NOT **BRAG**, AND IT IS NOT **PROUD**. LOVE IS NOT **RUDE**, IT IS NOT **SELFISH**, AND DOES NOT BECOME **ANGRY** EASILY. LOVE DOES NOT REMEMBER **WRONGS** DONE AGAINST IT. LOVE IS NOT **HAPPY** WITH EVIL, BUT IS HAPPY WITH **TRUTH**.

cont'd on next page...

18

...CONT'D FROM PREVIOUS PAGE.

LOVE PATIENTLY ACCEPTS ALL THINGS.
IT ALWAYS T R U S T S , ALWAYS
H O P E S , AND ALWAYS
CONTINUES S T R O N G . "

1 CORINTHIANS 13: 4-7

THIS IS LOVE

19

MATCH THE ANSWERS
MATCH THE ANSWERS ON THE FOLLOWING
PAGE TO THE QUESTIONS BELOW.

1. WHO SENT HIS SONS TO EGYPT TO
BUY GRAIN ?   GENESIS 42:1-2
   JACOB

2. WHO SAID TO JESUS, " YOU ARE THE CHRIST,
THE SON OF THE LIVING GOD "?   MATTHEW 16:16
   PETER

3. WHO SAID, " WHEN I NEEDED CLOTHES,
YOU CLOTHED ME " ?   MATTHEW 25:36
   JESUS

4. HOW MANY BOOKS IN THE BIBLE ARE
NAMED "JOHN" ?
   FOUR

5. ON WHICH DAY DID GOD CREATE THE
ANIMALS OF THE WATER AND THE AIR?
                          GENESIS 1:20-23
   FIFTH

6. WHAT ARE THE STORIES CALLED THAT
JESUS TAUGHT BY?   MATTHEW 13:13
   PARABLES

20

MATCH THE ANSWERS
MATCH THE ANSWERS ON THE FOLLOWING
PAGE TO THE QUESTIONS BELOW.

1. WHO SOLD HIS BIRTHRIGHT ?
   ESAU   GENESIS 25:29-34

2. WHO WAS JACOB TRICKED INTO
MARRYING ?   GENESIS 29: 20-25
   LEAH

3. WHAT OLD TESTAMENT COUPLE HAD
TWIN SONS ?   GENESIS 25: 20-26
   ISAAC & REBEKAH

4. WHOSE DAUGHTER DANCED AT HEROD'S
BIRTHDAY PARTY ?   MATTHEW 14:6
   HERODIAS'

5. WHAT DID SOLOMON HAVE SEVEN
HUNDRED OF ?   1 KINGS 11:3
   WIVES

6. ON THE ROAD TO WHAT CITY DID THE GOOD
SAMARITAN HELP THE BEATEN MAN ?   LUKE 10: 30-35
   JERICHO

22

MULTIPLE CHOICE
CIRCLE THE CORRECT ANSWER

1. WHO WAS MOSES' WIFE ?   EXODUS 2:21
   A. HAGAR
   (B) ZIPPORAH
   C. REBEKAH

2. WHO WAS THE FIRST PRIEST OF ISRAEL?
                              EXODUS 28:1
   A. ABRAHAM
   B. MOSES
   (C) AARON

3. WHO WAS A JUDGE FOR THE PEOPLE OF
ISRAEL FOR TWENTY YEARS ?   JUDGES 16:31
   A. SAUL
   (B) SAMSON
   C. DAVID

CONT'D NEXT PAGE...

24

...CONT'D FROM PREVIOUS PAGE.

4. WHO PREACHED IN THE WILDERNESS OF
JUDEA ?   MATTHEW 3:1
   A. JOHN
   B. JESUS
   (C) JOHN THE BAPTIST

5. WHAT WAS THE NAME OF MARY'S SISTER
WHO WORKED HARD IN THE KITCHEN?
                              LUKE 10:40
   A. RUTH
   B. DEBORAH
   (C) MARTHA

6. WHO WROTE THE BOOK OF REVELATION?
                              REVELATION 1:4
   A. PAUL
   (B) JOHN
   C. PETER

25

MATCH THE ANSWERS
MATCH THE ANSWERS ON THE FOLLOWING
PAGE TO THE QUESTIONS BELOW.

1. HOW OLD WAS ABRAHAM WHEN ISAAC
WAS BORN ?   GENESIS 21:5
   ONE HUNDRED

2. HOW MANY DAYS WAS SAUL BLIND ?
   THREE   ACTS 9:9

3. WHAT COMMANDMENT IS "HONOR YOUR
FATHER AND YOUR MOTHER" ? EXODUS 20:12
   FIFTH

4. WHAT DOES "GENESIS" MEAN ?
   BEGINNING

5. WHAT LANGUAGE WAS THE NEW
TESTAMENT WRITTEN IN ?
   GREEK

6. WHAT NEW TESTAMENT BOOK TELLS
OF JESUS GOING UP TO HEAVEN ?
   ACTS

26

FILL IN THE BLANKS

WORD LIST	
STAND	DOOR
KNOCK	ANYONE
VOICE	OPENS
EAT	HE

" HERE I AM ! I S T A N D AT
THE D O O R AND K N O C K .
IF A N Y O N E HEARS MY
V O I C E AND O P E N S
THE DOOR, I WILL COME IN AND
E A T WITH HIM, AND H E
WILL EAT WITH ME."
                     REVELATION 3:20

28

FILL IN THE BLANKS

WORD LIST	
ASK	KNOCK
SEARCH	OPEN
FIND	GOD
YOU	DOOR

" CONTINUE TO A S K AND G O D
WILL GIVE TO YOU. CONTINUE TO
S E A R C H AND Y O U
WILL F I N D . CONTINUE TO
K N O C K AND THE D O O R
WILL BE O P E N FOR YOU."
                     MATTHEW 7:7

29

MULTIPLE CHOICE
CIRCLE THE CORRECT ANSWER.

1. WHO WAS TAKEN OUT OF SODOM BEFORE
IT WAS DESTROYED ?   GENESIS 19:15
   A. ABRAHAM AND HIS FAMILY
   (B) LOT AND HIS FAMILY
   C. ISAAC AND HIS FAMILY

2. WHO WAS ISAAC'S FATHER ?   GENESIS 21:3
   A. JACOB
   B. NOAH
   (C) ABRAHAM

3. WHO WAS SARAI'S MAID?   GENESIS 16:1
   A. REBEKAH
   (B) HAGAR
   C. RUTH

CONT'D NEXT PAGE...

30

...cont'd from previous page.

4. JESUS RAISED LAZARUS FROM THE DEAD. WHO WERE LAZARUS' SISTERS?
John 11:1-3

   A. MARY AND ELIZABETH

   B. RUTH AND NAOMI

   Ⓒ MARTHA AND MARY

5. WHAT DID JESUS SAY HE WOULD BUILD HIS CHURCH ON?
Matthew 16:18

   A. THIS MOUNTAIN

   B. THIS HILL

   Ⓒ THIS ROCK

6. WHAT DID JUDAS DO AFTER HE BETRAYED JESUS?
Matthew 27:5

   A. SAID SORRY

   B. CRIED

   Ⓒ HANGED HIMSELF

31

MULTIPLE CHOICE
CIRCLE THE CORRECT ANSWER.

1. WHAT DOES TESTAMENT MEAN?

   A. TO TEST

   Ⓑ AGREEMENT

   C. BOOKS

2. WHAT DID THE ISRAELITES PUT ON THEIR DOOR POSTS SO THAT THE DEATH ANGEL WOULD PASS BY?
Exodus 12:21-23

   A. GOAT'S BLOOD

   B. PAINT

   Ⓒ LAMB'S BLOOD

3. WHAT ARE WE TO POUR ON THE SICK SO THAT THE PRAYER OF FAITH WILL MAKE THEM WELL?
James 5:14

   A. MEDICINE

   B. WATER

   Ⓒ OIL

cont'd next page...

32

...cont'd from previous page.

4. WHAT ARE WE SUPPOSED TO DO WHEN WE SIN?
James 5:16

   A. FORGET ABOUT IT

   Ⓑ CONFESS IT TO EACH OTHER

   C. PRETEND IT DIDN'T HAPPEN

5. JESUS CALLED MATTHEW TO BE A DISCIPLE. WHAT WAS HE BEFORE JESUS CALLED HIM?
Matthew 9:9

   A. A FISHERMAN

   Ⓑ A TAX COLLECTOR

   C. A BASE BALL PLAYER

6. WHAT DID JESUS SAY HE WOULD MAKE PETER AND ANDREW?
Mark 1:16-17

   A. SINGERS

   B. KINGS

   Ⓒ FISHERS OF MEN

33

MATCH THE ANSWERS
MATCH THE ANSWERS ON THE FOLLOWING PAGE TO THE QUESTIONS BELOW.

1. IN THE ARMOR OF GOD, WHAT IS THE SHIELD CALLED?
FAITH
Ephesians 6:16

2. WHAT IS THE HELMET CALLED?
SALVATION
Ephesians 6:17

3. WHAT IS THE SWORD CALLED?
WORD OF GOD
Ephesians 6:17

4. WHAT IS THE BELT CALLED?
TRUTH
Ephesians 6:14

5. WHAT INGREDIENT IN THE KITCHEN DID JESUS SAY WE WERE LIKE?
SALT
Matthew 5:13

6. WHAT BOOK OF THE BIBLE HAS THE MOST CHAPTERS?
PSALMS

34

MATCH THE ANSWERS
MATCH THE ANSWERS ON THE FOLLOWING PAGE TO THE QUESTIONS BELOW.

1. IN THE DESERT, GOD GAVE THE ISRAELITES MANNA TO EAT. WHAT ELSE DID GOD GIVE THEM?
QUAILS
Exodus 16:13

2. WHAT DOES JESUS GIVE TO THOSE WHO CHOOSE TO FOLLOW HIM?
ETERNAL LIFE
John 10:27-28

3. WHAT SPECIAL DAY WAS IT WHEN THE BELIEVERS RECEIVED THE HOLY SPIRIT?
PENTECOST
Acts 2:1-4

4. A MAN REAPS WHAT HE ... WHAT?
SOWS
Galatians 6:7

5. WHAT DID JESUS SAY HE HAD OVERCOME?
WORLD
John 16:33

6. IN WHAT COUNTRY DID ISAAC FIND A WIFE?
MESOPOTAMIA
Genesis 24:4, 10

36

FILL IN THE BLANKS

WORD LIST	
PERSON	JESUS
LIVE	BREAD
EATING	BY
EVERYTHING	LORD

" **JESUS** SAID, ' A **PERSON** DOES NOT **LIVE** ONLY BY **EATING** **BREAD**, BUT A PERSON LIVES **BY EVERYTHING** THE **LORD** SAYS ' "
Matthew 4:4

38

FILL IN THE BLANKS

WORD LIST	
BEGINS	RESPECT
WISDOM	LORD
KNOWLEDGE	FOOLISH
SELF-CONTROL	

" **KNOWLEDGE** **BEGINS** WITH **RESPECT** FOR THE **LORD**, BUT **FOOLISH** PEOPLE HATE **WISDOM** AND **SELF**-**CONTROL**. "
Proverbs 1:7

39

FILL IN THE BLANKS

WORD LIST	
LOVE	KINDNESS
JOY	FAITHFULNESS
SELF-CONTROL	PEACE
GENTLENESS	PATIENCE
GOODNESS	

" BUT THE SPIRIT GIVES **LOVE**, **JOY**, **PEACE**, **PATIENCE**, **KINDNESS**, **GOODNESS**, **FAITHFULNESS**, **GENTLENESS**, AND **SELF**-**CONTROL**. THERE IS NO LAW THAT SAYS THESE THINGS ARE WRONG. "
Galatians 5:22-23

40

FILL IN THE BLANKS

WORD LIST	
HELPER	EVERYTHING
NAME	YOU
HOLY	REMEMBER
FATHER	HE

" BUT THE **HELPER** WILL TEACH YOU **EVERYTHING**. **HE** WILL CAUSE YOU TO **REMEMBER** ALL THE THINGS I TOLD **YOU**. THIS HELPER IS THE **HOLY** SPIRIT WHOM THE **FATHER** WILL SEND IN MY **NAME**. "
John 14:26

41

MATCH THE ANSWERS

MATCH THE ANSWERS ON THE FOLLOWING PAGE TO THE QUESTIONS BELOW.

1. IN THE PARABLE OF THE TALENTS, HOW MANY SERVANTS WERE GIVEN TALENTS?
THREE _Matthew 25:14-15_

2. HOW OLD WAS JAIRUS' DAUGHTER WHEN SHE GOT SICK?
TWELVE _Luke 8:1-2_

3. HOW MANY MIRACLES, OR "SIGNS", DID JESUS GIVE TO THE PHARISEES?
EIGHT _Matthew 27:15-26_

4. HOW MANY WIVES DID JACOB HAVE?
FOUR _Genesis 29:21-30_

5. HOW MANY PIECES OF SILVER WAS JUDAS PAID TO BETRAY JESUS?
THIRTY _Matthew 26:15_

6. HOW MANY CONCUBINES DID KING SOLOMON HAVE?
THREE HUNDRED _1 Kings 11:3_

42

... CONT'D FROM PREVIOUS PAGE.

4. WHO WAS THE COUSIN OF MORDECAI THAT BECAME A QUEEN? _Esther 2:15-17_
   A. RUTH
   B. NAOMI
   Ⓒ ESTHER

5. WHO WROTE THE RIDDLE ABOUT THE LION? _Judges 14:16-18_
   A. JUDGES
   B. SOLOMON
   Ⓒ SAMSON

6. WHO CALLED DOWN FIRE FROM HEAVEN? _2 Kings 1:10_
   A. ELISHA
   Ⓑ ELIJAH
   C. JEREMIAH

47

MULTIPLE CHOICE

CIRCLE THE CORRECT ANSWER.

1. WHAT DID JESUS TELL THE DISCIPLES TO DO IF THEY WERE NOT WELCOME AT SOMEONE'S HOME? _Matthew 10:14_
   A. GET ANGRY.
   B. WHINE AND CRY.
   Ⓒ SHAKE THE DUST OFF YOUR FEET.

2. WHAT WAS JOHN THE BAPTIST'S CLOTHING MADE OF? _Matthew 3:4_
   A. SILK
   B. WOOL
   Ⓒ CAMEL'S HAIR

3. WHAT KIND OF CROWN WILL JESUS GIVE US IF WE ARE FAITHFUL TO THE END? _Revelation 2:10_
   A. CROWN OF GOLD
   B. CROWN OF SILVER
   Ⓒ CROWN OF LIFE

CONT'D NEXT PAGE ...

50

MATCH THE ANSWERS

MATCH THE ANSWERS ON THE FOLLOWING PAGE TO THE QUESTIONS BELOW.

1. HOW MANY WERE AT THE LAST SUPPER WITH JESUS? _Matthew 26:19-20_
TWELVE

2. HOW LONG IS A MILLENNIUM? _Revelation 20:4,6,7_
ONE THOUSAND YEARS

3. WHICH OLD TESTAMENT BOOK TELLS ABOUT THE LIFE OF ABRAHAM?
GENESIS

4. WHAT PEOPLE WANTED TO KNOW THE SECRET OF SAMSON'S STRENGTH? _Judges 16:4-5_
PHILISTINES

5. WHO WAS THE ONLY FEMALE JUDGE OF ISRAEL? _Judges 4:4-16_
DEBORAH

6. THE LORD SAID HE IS THE ALPHA AND THE OMEGA. WHAT DOES OMEGA MEAN? _Revelation 22:13_
LAST, END

44

MULTIPLE CHOICE

CIRCLE THE CORRECT ANSWER.

1. WHAT EXCUSE DID MOSES GIVE TO GOD FOR WHY HE DIDN'T WANT TO GO TO EGYPT? _Exodus 4:10_
   A. "I'M TOO TIRED."
   B. "I HAVE OTHER PLANS."
   Ⓒ "I AM SLOW TO SPEAK."

2. WHAT DID JOSEPH INTERPRET FOR PHARAOH? _Genesis 41:14-36_
   A. HIS WIFE'S DREAMS
   B. A RECIPE FOR PUDDING
   Ⓒ HIS DREAMS

3. JESUS SAID THAT WHEN HE RETURNS AGAIN, HE WILL COME LIKE A ___ WHAT? _Revelation 16:15_
   A. FLASH OF LIGHTNING
   B. BOLT OF THUNDER
   Ⓒ THIEF IN THE NIGHT

CONT'D NEXT PAGE ...

48

... CONT'D FROM PREVIOUS PAGE.

4. WHAT ARE WE TOLD TO TAKE UP TO FOLLOW JESUS? _Matthew 10:38_
   A. OUR SUITCASES
   Ⓑ OUR CROSSES
   C. OUR COATS

5. FAITH WITHOUT WORKS IS DEAD? _James 2:20_
   A. WORDS
   Ⓑ WORKS
   C. WISDOM

6. WHAT DID DANIEL AND HIS FRIENDS REFUSE TO EAT AND DRINK AT THE KING'S TABLE? _Daniel 1:8_
   A. LIVER, ONIONS, AND CARROT JUICE
   Ⓑ MEAT AND WINE
   C. PIZZA AND SODA

51

CONT'D NEXT PAGE ...

MULTIPLE CHOICE

CIRCLE THE CORRECT ANSWER.

1. WHO WAS JOSEPH'S MOTHER? _Genesis 30:22-24_
   A. LEAH
   Ⓑ RACHEL
   C. REBEKAH

2. WHO WAS THE FIRST KING OF ISRAEL? _1 Samuel 10:20-25_
   A. AARON
   B. DAVID
   Ⓒ SAUL

3. WHAT WAS BELTESHAZZAR'S OTHER NAME? _Daniel 1:7_
   A. SIMON
   Ⓑ DANIEL
   C. JOB

CONT'D NEXT PAGE ...

46

... CONT'D FROM PREVIOUS PAGE.

4. WHAT DID THE WOMEN BRING TO JESUS' TOMB? _Mark 16:1_
   A. FLOWERS
   Ⓑ SWEET SPICES
   C. PEOPLE

5. WHAT DID ESAU DO FOR A LIVING? _Genesis 25:27_
   A. FARM
   B. BUILD
   Ⓒ HUNT

6. IN THE PARABLE OF THE SOWER, WHAT DOES THE SEED STAND FOR? _Luke 8:11_
   A. A PLANT
   B. CORN
   Ⓒ THE WORD OF GOD

49

FILL IN THE BLANKS

WORD LIST	
TRUST	EVERYTHING
SUCCESS	OWN
HEART	REMEMBER
DEPEND	LORD

* **TRUST** IN THE **LORD** WITH ALL YOUR **HEART**. DON'T **DEPEND** ON YOUR **OWN** UNDERSTANDING. **REMEMBER** THE LORD IN **EVERYTHING** YOU DO. AND HE WILL GIVE YOU **SUCCESS**! _Proverbs 3:5-6_

52

FILL IN THE BLANKS

WORD LIST
DEPEND	SUN
NOONDAY	LORD
FAIRNESS	GOODNESS
HE	CARE

" <u>DEPEND</u> ON THE <u>LORD</u>
TRUST HIM AND <u>HE</u> WILL TAKE
<u>CARE</u> OF YOU. THEN YOUR
<u>GOODNESS</u> WILL
SHINE LIKE THE <u>SUN</u>. YOUR
<u>FAIRNESS</u> WILL SHINE
LIKE THE <u>NOONDAY</u> SUN. "

PSALM 37:5,6

53

FILL IN THE BLANKS

WORD LIST
WAIT	LEADS
TRUST	RICH
LORD	ANGRY
UPSET	TROUBLE

" <u>WAIT</u> AND <u>TRUST</u>
THE <u>LORD</u>. DON'T BE
<u>UPSET</u> WHEN OTHERS
GET <u>RICH</u> OR WHEN
SOMEONE ELSE'S PLANS SUCCEED.
DON'T GET <u>ANGRY</u>. DON'T
BE UPSET, IT ONLY <u>LEADS</u>
TO <u>TROUBLE</u>. "

PSALM 37:7,8

54

FILL IN THE BLANKS

WORD LIST
EAT	ROARING
CAREFUL	CONTROL
DEVIL	LOOKING
HE	ENEMY

" <u>CONTROL</u> YOURSELVES
AND BE <u>CAREFUL</u>.
THE <u>DEVIL</u> IS YOUR
<u>ENEMY</u> AND <u>HE</u> GOES
AROUND LIKE A <u>ROARING</u>
LION <u>LOOKING</u> FOR
SOMEONE TO <u>EAT</u> "

1 PETER 5:8

YUM!
YUM!

55

MATCH THE ANSWERS

MATCH THE ANSWERS ON THE FOLLOWING
PAGE TO THE QUESTIONS BELOW.

1. WHO DID ISAAC BLESS INSTEAD OF
ESAU ?
<u>JACOB</u>   GENESIS 27:22-29

2. WHO TOLD THE BROTHERS OF JOSEPH NOT
TO HARM JOSEPH ?
<u>REUBEN</u>   GENESIS 37:22

3. WHO SAID THEY SHOULD SELL JOSEPH
RATHER THAN KILL HIM ?
<u>JUDAH</u>   GENESIS 37:26-27

4. WHO HAD A DREAM ABOUT THE SUN,
MOON, AND STARS BOWING DOWN TO
HIM ?
<u>JOSEPH</u>   GENESIS 37:9-11

5. WHO PURCHASED JOSEPH AS A SLAVE ?
<u>POTIPHAR</u>   GENESIS 37:36

6. WHO WAS JOSEPH'S MOTHER ?
<u>RACHEL</u>   GENESIS 30:22-24

56

MATCH THE ANSWERS

MATCH THE ANSWERS ON THE FOLLOWING
PAGE TO THE QUESTIONS BELOW.

1. WHO WAS THE FATHER OF JAMES
AND JOHN ?
<u>ZEBEDEE</u>   LUKE 5:10

2. WHAT TWO DISCIPLES FOLLOWED
JESUS FIRST ?
<u>SIMON PETER & ANDREW</u> MATTHEW 4:18

3. HOW MANY BOOKS IN THE NEW
TESTAMENT HAVE ONLY ONE CHAPTER ?
<u>FOUR</u>

4. THE FOUR GOSPELS ARE ABOUT WHOM ?
<u>JESUS</u>

5. WHAT DO WE CALL THE DAY IN WHICH WE
REMEMBER JESUS' DEATH ON THE
CROSS ?
<u>GOOD FRIDAY</u>

6. WHICH DISCIPLE WAS SENT TO THE ISLAND
OF PATMOS ?
<u>JOHN</u>   REVELATION 1:9

58

MULTIPLE CHOICE

CIRCLE THE CORRECT ANSWER.

1. ON WHAT WAS JOHN THE BAPTIST'S HEAD
PUT TO GIVE TO HERODIAS' DAUGHTER ?
MATTHEW 14:8
   A. STICK
   (B.) PLATTER
   C. BOWL

2. WHAT HAPPENED TO THE MEN THAT
THREW SHADRACH, MESHACH, AND
ABEDNEGO INTO THE FIERY FURNACE ?
DANIEL 3:22
   A. THEIR HAIR WAS SINGED
   (B.) THE HEAT OF THE FIRE
       KILLED THEM.
   C. THEY GOT VERY WARM.

3. WHAT DOES JAMES SAY SHALL SAVE
THE SICK ? JAMES 5:15
   A. A DOCTOR
   B. GOING TO THE HOSPITAL
   (C.) A PRAYER OF FAITH

60

... CONT'D FROM PREVIOUS PAGE.

4. WHAT WAS JOHN THE BAPTIST UNWORTHY
TO UNTIE ? MARK 1:7
   A. JESUS' NECKTIE
   B. JESUS' CLOAK
   C. JESUS' SANDALS

5. WHY DID MARY AND JOSEPH GO TO
BETHLEHEM ? LUKE 2:1-4
   A. FOR A VACATION
   (B.) TO REGISTER THEIR
       NAMES TO PAY TAXES
   C. TO VISIT ELIZABETH

6. WHAT HAPPENED TO THE WATERS OF
MARAH WHEN MOSES THREW A TREE IN ?
EXODUS 15:23-25
   A. THE TREE BLOCKED THE WATER.
   (B.) MADE THE WATER SWEET
       OR GOOD TO DRINK
   C. MADE A MESS

61

MULTIPLE CHOICE

CIRCLE THE CORRECT ANSWER

1. WHAT WAS GIVEN TO PAUL TO KEEP HIM
HUMBLE ? 2 CORINTHIANS 12:7
   (A.) A THORN IN THE FLESH
   B. BLINDNESS
   C. POVERTY

2. FOR WHAT DID ESAU SELL HIS
BIRTHRIGHT ? GENESIS 25:34
   A. HAMBURGER AND FRIES
   (B.) A BOWL OF STEW
   C. A NEW SUIT OF CLOTHES

3. WHAT DID JESUS SAY THE RICH MAN
MUST SELL TO HAVE TREASURES IN
HEAVEN ? MATTHEW 19:21
   A. HIS HOUSE
   (B.) ALL HIS POSSESSIONS
   C. HIS BROTHER

62

CONT'D FROM PREVIOUS PAGE.

4. WHAT WAS FOUND IN BENJAMIN'S
PACK ? GENESIS 44:12
   A. A FROG
   B. HIS CLOTHES
   (C.) JOSEPH'S SILVER CUP

5. WHAT KIND OF TREE DID JESUS
CONDEMN ? MATTHEW 21:19
   A. AN APPLE TREE
   (B.) A FIG TREE
   C. A PLUM TREE

6. WHAT PARABLE TELLS OF THE SON THAT
LEAVES HOME AND WASTES ALL HIS
MONEY ? LUKE 15:11-32
   A. THE STUBBORN SON
   B. THE FIRST SON
   (C.) THE PRODIGAL SON

OUCH!

63

FILL IN THE BLANKS

WORD LIST

DEEPLY	HOMES
LOOKING	OTHERS'
COMPLAINING	EACH
OPEN	LOVE

" MOST IMPORTANTLY __LOVE__
EACH OTHER __DEEPLY__.
LOVE HAS A WAY OF NOT
__LOOKING__ AT __OTHERS'__
SINS __OPEN__ YOUR
__HOMES__ TO __EACH__
OTHER WITHOUT
__COMPLAINING__."

1 PETER 4:8-9

64

FILL IN THE BLANKS

WORD LIST

GIFT	GRACE
DIFFERENT	RESPONSIBLE
SERVANTS	YOU
GOD'S	EACH

" __EACH__ OF YOU RECEIVED A
SPIRITUAL __GIFT__. GOD HAS
SHOWN YOU HIS __GRACE__
IN GIVING YOU __DIFFERENT__
GIFTS AND __YOU__ ARE LIKE
__SERVANTS__ WHO ARE
__RESPONSIBLE__
FOR USING __GOD'S__ GIFTS "

1 PETER 4:10

65

READ 2 PETER 1:5-7. WHAT SHOULD YOU
ADD TO EACH QUALITY BELOW?

LOOK ON THE FOLLOWING PAGE FOR
YOUR ANSWERS.

FAITH	__GOODNESS__
GOODNESS	__KNOWLEDGE__
KNOWLEDGE	__SELF-CONTROL__
SELF-CONTROL	__ABILITY TO HOLD ON__
ABILITY TO HOLD ON	__SERVICE TO GOD__
SERVICE TO GOD	__BROTHERLY KINDNESS__
BROTHERLY KINDNESS	__LOVE__

THIS SCRIPTURE CONTINUES IN VERSES 8-9.

" IF ALL THESE THINGS ARE IN YOU AND ARE
GROWING, THEY WILL HELP YOU NEVER TO
BE USELESS. THEY WILL HELP YOUR
KNOWLEDGE OF OUR LORD JESUS CHRIST
AND MAKE YOUR LIVES BETTER. BUT IF
ANYONE DOES NOT HAVE THESE THINGS,
HE CANNOT SEE CLEARLY. HE IS BLIND.
HE HAS FORGOTTEN THAT HE WAS MADE
CLEAN FROM HIS PAST SINS."

WHAT A GREAT PROMISE!

66

MATCH THE COLUMNS

WHO WAS WHOSE WIFE?

DRAW A LINE TO MATCH HUSBAND
TO WIFE.

ABRAHAM	RUTH
BOAZ	PRISCILLA
DAVID	HERODIAS
KING XERXES	BATHSHEBA
ELKANAH	ESTHER
HEROD	HANNAH
AQUILA	SARAH

68

TRUE / FALSE

1. JOSEPH WAS TWENTY-THREE YEARS
OLD WHEN HIS BROTHERS SOLD HIM
TO THE ISHMAELITES

GENESIS 37:2   TRUE ___   FALSE ✓

2. LAZARUS HAD BEEN DEAD FOR THREE
DAYS WHEN JESUS CALLED HIM OUT OF
HIS TOMB, RAISING HIM TO LIFE.

JOHN 11:39   TRUE ___   FALSE ✓

3. MOSES AND ABRAHAM APPEARED
WITH JESUS ON THE MOUNT OF
TRANSFIGURATION.

MATTHEW 17:3   TRUE ___   FALSE ✓

4. JESUS FED FOUR THOUSAND PEOPLE
WITH A FEW LOAVES OF BREAD AND
SOME FISH.

MATTHEW 15:32-38   TRUE ✓   FALSE ___

69

MULTIPLE CHOICE

CIRCLE THE CORRECT ANSWER.

1. HE WANTED TO PUT HIS HAND IN JESUS' SIDE
AFTER THE RESURRECTION.   JOHN 20:24-30

  (A) THOMAS
  B. JOHN
  C. PETER

2. JESUS CALLED HIM AWAY FROM HIS
JOB AS A TAX COLLECTOR   MATTHEW 9:9

  A. PHILIP
  (B) MATTHEW
  C. JAMES

3. JESUS HEALED HIS MOTHER-IN-LAW   MATTHEW 8:14-15

  A. JOHN
  B. JAMES
  (C) PETER

CON'D NEXT PAGE...

70

...CONT'D FROM PREVIOUS PAGE.

4. HE GAVE JESUS A KISS, BUT NOT OUT
OF LOVE.

  A. PONTIUS PILATE
  (D) JUDAS ISCARIOT
  C. JOHN

5. HE BAPTIZED AN ETHIOPIAN HE MET
ON THE ROAD.   ACTS 8:26-39

  (A) PHILIP
  B. SIMON
  C. ANDREW

6. HE AND HIS BROTHER LEFT THEIR
FATHER TO FOLLOW JESUS.   MATTHEW 4:18

  (A) PETER
  B. THOMAS
  C. JUDAS

71

FINISH THE VERSE

HERE ARE SOME OF THE BEATITUDES.
FINISH THEM BY MATCHING THEM WITH
THE PHRASES ON THE FOLLOWING PAGE.

1. " BLESSED ARE THE POOR IN SPIRIT."
__"THEIRS IS THE KINGDOM OF HEAVEN."__

2. " BLESSED ARE THOSE WHO MOURN."
__"THEY WILL BE COMFORTED."__

3. " BLESSED ARE THE MEEK."
__"THEY WILL INHERIT THE EARTH."__

4. " BLESSED ARE THOSE WHO HUNGER AND
THIRST FOR RIGHTEOUSNESS."
__"THEY WILL BE FILLED."__

5. " BLESSED ARE THE MERCIFUL."
__"THEY WILL BE SHOWN MERCY."__

6. " BLESSED ARE THE PEACEMAKERS."
__" THEY WILL BE CALLED SONS OF GOD."__

MATTHEW 5:1-10
(NEW INTERNATIONAL VERSION)

72

MATCH THE SAYING

MATCH THE SAYING BELOW WITH THE
PERSON WHO SAID IT FROM THE
FOLLOWING PAGE.

1. " YOUR FATHER AND I WERE VERY
WORRIED ABOUT YOU. WE HAVE BEEN
LOOKING FOR YOU."   LUKE 2:48
__MARY, HIS MOTHER__

2. " I SINNED I GAVE AN
INNOCENT MAN TO BE KILLED."   MATTHEW 27:4
__JUDAS ISCARIOT__

3. " AS FOR ME AND MY FAMILY, WE WILL
SERVE THE LORD."   JOSHUA 24:14-15
__JOSHUA__

4. " NO! I WANT CAESAR TO HEAR MY
CASE!"   ACTS 25:10-11
__PAUL__

5. " I HAVE SINNED AGAINST THE
LORD."   2 SAMUEL 12:13
__DAVID__

74

IN THE BLANKS

R2I	
VER	MORNING
	CRY
	YOU
	VOICE

TO MY **C R Y** FOR

MY KING AND MY **G O D**,

TO **Y O U**. LORD,

M O R N I N G YOU

MY **V O I C E**.

MORNING I TELL YOU

I **N E E D**. AND

I T FOR YOUR

WER."   PSALM 5:2-3

76

FILL IN THE BLANKS

WORD LIST	
TIRED	WORK
HEAVY	SOULS
REST	EASY
LOADS	LEARN

" COME TO ME, ALL OF YOU WHO
ARE **T I R E D** AND HAVE
HEAVY **L O A D S**. I WILL
GIVE YOU **R E S T**. ACCEPT
MY **W O R K** AND **L E A R N**
FROM ME. I AM GENTLE AND
HUMBLE IN SPIRIT. AND YOU
WILL FIND REST FOR YOUR
S O U L S. THE WORK I
ASK YOU TO ACCEPT IS
E A S Y. THE LOAD I
GIVE YOU TO CARRY IS NOT
H E A V Y. "

MATTHEW 11:28-30

77

MULTIPLE CHOICE
CIRCLE THE CORRECT ANSWER.

1. HOW MANY TIMES DID JOSEPH AND
MARY RUN FOR THEIR LIVES WITH JESUS?   MATTHEW 2:14-21

   A) ONCE

   B. TWICE

   C. THREE TIMES

2. HOW MANY DAYS DID GOD GIVE THE
PEOPLE OF NINEVEH TO TURN FROM
THEIR SIN OR THEY WOULD BE
DESTROYED?   JONAH 3:4

   A. SEVEN DAYS

   B) FORTY DAYS

   C. TWENTY DAYS

3. HOW LONG DID IT GO ON WITHOUT
RAINING AFTER ELIJAH PRAYED?   LUKE 4:25

   A. TWO AND A HALF DAYS

   B. THREE AND A HALF DAYS

   C) THREE AND A HALF YEARS

CONT'D NEXT PAGE...

78

...CONT'D FROM PREVIOUS PAGE...

MANY PEOPLE DID KING
CHADNEZZAR SEE WALKING IN
URNACE ?   DANIEL 3:25

   A. THREE

   B) FOUR

   C. FIVE

MANY BROTHERS DID JESUS
?   MARK 6:3

   A. NONE

   B. TWO

   C) FOUR

N PLAGUE ON EGYPT INVOLVED
AND FIRE ?   EXODUS 9:23-26

   A. THE THIRD

   B. THE FIFTH

   C) THE SEVENTH

79

MULTIPLE CHOICE
CIRCLE THE CORRECT ANSWER.

1. HOW OLD WAS JESUS WHEN HE WAS
BAPTIZED AND STARTED HIS MINISTRY?   LUKE 3:21-23

   A. ABOUT NINETEEN

   B. ABOUT TWENTY-FIVE

   C) ABOUT THIRTY

2. HOW LONG WAS MOSES ON THE
MOUNTAIN TO RECEIVE THE TEN
COMMANDMENTS ?   EXODUS 24:18

   A. OVERNIGHT

   B. FORTY DAYS

   C) FORTY DAYS AND NIGHTS

3. WHEN HE WAS PRAYING, HOW MANY
TIMES DID JESUS WAKE HIS DISCIPLES
IN THE GARDEN OF GETHSEMANE ?   MATTHEW 26:36-45

   A. ONCE

   B. TWICE

   C) THREE TIMES

CONT'D NEXT PAGE...

80

---

4. WHAT PIECE OF CLOTHING DID THE
SOLDIERS MAKE JESUS WEAR?   JOHN 19:1-2

   A. A WHITE ROBE

   B) A PURPLE ROBE

   C. A BLUE ROBE

5. WHAT WOMAN LED AN ARMY INTO
BATTLE ?   JUDGES 4:6-7

   A. RUTH

   B) DEBORAH

   C. ESTHER

6. WHAT OTHER NAME WERE THE WISE
MEN CALLED ?   MATTHEW 2:1

   A. SMART MEN

   B. KINGS

   C) MAGI

81

CH THE ANSWERS
ME ANSWERS ON THE FOLLOWING
THE QUESTIONS BELOW.

THIRD MISSIONARY JOURNEY,
WAS PAUL ARRESTED?
SALEM   ACTS 21:10-33

NY BASKETS OF BREAD WERE
FTER JESUS FED THE FOUR
ND ?   MATTHEW 15:34-37
BASKETS

OUGHT DORCAS, A DISCIPLE IN
BACK TO LIFE ?
ER   ACTS 9:36-41

O KING DAVID SEND TO THE
LINE SO THAT HE WOULD BE
IN BATTLE ?   2 SAMUEL 11:14-17
AH

WANTED JESUS' TOMB SEALED AND
ED SO NO ONE COULD STEAL THE
CISEES   MATTHEW 27:62-66

HREATENED TO KILL ALL THE
ERS OF JESUS ?   ACTS 9:1
L

82

TRUE / FALSE

1. THE BOOK OF EXODUS RECORDS THAT
JOSEPH DIED WHEN HE WAS ONE
HUNDRED AND TEN YEARS OLD.
GENESIS 50:26   TRUE ___ FALSE ✓

2. MOSES WAS ABRAHAM'S FATHER.
NUMBERS 26:59   TRUE ___ FALSE ✓

3. HAM, THE SON OF NOAH, HAD FOUR
SONS.
GENESIS 10:6   TRUE ✓ FALSE ___

4. PONTIUS PILATE ORDERED THREE
SOLDIERS TO GUARD JESUS' TOMB.
MATTHEW 27:66   TRUE ___ FALSE ✓

5. JONATHAN WAS SAMUEL'S SON.
1 SAMUEL 14:49   TRUE ___ FALSE ✓

84

TRUE / FALSE

1. JESUS WAS BORN IN JERUSALEM.
MATTHEW 2:1   TRUE ___ FALSE ✓

2. THE THREE WISE MEN RETURNED
TO KING HEROD WITH INFORMATION
ABOUT JESUS.
MATTHEW 2:12   TRUE ___ FALSE ✓

3. JESUS WAS CALLED A NAZARENE
BECAUSE HE LIVED IN THE TOWN OF
NAZARETH.
MATTHEW 2:23   TRUE ✓ FALSE ___

4. PETER BETRAYED JESUS AS THE LORD
HAD SAID HE WOULD.
JOHN 13:36   TRUE ___ FALSE ✓

5. GOLIATH WAS AN ISRAELITE AND A
FRIEND OF THE YOUNG DAVID.
1 SAMUEL 17:4   TRUE ___ FALSE ✓

85

TRUE / FALSE

1. KING SAUL WANTED TO KILL DAVID
   BECAUSE OF HIS JEALOUSY.
   1 SAMUEL 19:1   TRUE ✓ FALSE ___

2. NOAH LIVED FOR NINE HUNDRED
   AND THIRTY-FIVE YEARS.
   GENESIS 9:29   TRUE ___ FALSE ✓

3. AT FIRST, JOSEPH FELT HE SHOULD
   DIVORCE MARY WHEN HE FOUND OUT
   SHE WAS PREGNANT.
   MATTHEW 1:19   TRUE ✓ FALSE ___

4. JESUS' FATHER, JOSEPH, WAS A
   SON OF DAVID.
   MATTHEW 1:20   TRUE ✓ FALSE ___

5. EMMANUEL MEANS "GOD WITH US"
   AND IS ANOTHER NAME FOR JESUS
   FROM THE OLD TESTAMENT.
   MATTHEW 1:23   TRUE ✓ FALSE ___
   ISAIAH 7:14

86

MULTIPLE CHOICE
CIRCLE THE CORRECT ANSWER.

1. WHO WAS JACOB'S FIRST SON?
   GENESIS 49:3
   A. ESAU
   (B) REUBEN
   C. ISAAC

2. HOW MANY SONS DID TERAH HAVE?
   GENESIS 11:26
   A. ONE
   B. TWO
   (C) THREE

3. WHAT WAS NIMROD KNOWN AS?
   GENESIS 10:9
   A. A GREAT WARRIOR
   B. A GREAT FARMER
   (C) A GREAT HUNTER

CONT'D NEXT PAGE...

90

MATCH THE SAYING

MATCH THE SAYING BELOW WITH THE
PERSON WHO SAID IT FROM THE
FOLLOWING PAGE.

1. " THIS PUNISHMENT IS MORE THAN
   I CAN STAND! "   GENESIS 4:13
   CAIN

2. " THERE IS ONLY ONE GOD AND THERE
   IS ONLY ONE WAY THAN PEOPLE CAN
   REACH GOD. "   1 TIMOTHY
   2:5
   PAUL

3. " BUT THE MOST HIGH DOES NOT LIVE IN
   HOUSES THAT MEN BUILD WITH THEIR HANDS! "
   STEPHEN   ACTS 7:48
   7:48

4. " SEE, TODAY I AM LETTING YOU CHOOSE A
   BLESSING OR A CURSE. "   DEUTERONOMY 11:26
   11:26
   MOSES

5. " AS SURELY AS THE LORD LIVES, DAVID
   WON'T BE PUT TO DEATH. "   1 SAMUEL 19:6
   SAUL

87

...CONT'D FROM PREVIOUS PAGE.

4. WHAT WAS THE NAME OF SAMUEL'S
   FIRSTBORN SON?   1 SAMUEL 8:2
   A. ABIJAH
   (B) JOEL
   C. SAMUEL, JR.

5. HOW DID PETER ESCAPE FROM
   PRISON?   ACTS 12:7-10
   A. HE DRILLED HIS WAY OUT.
   B. HIS FRIENDS HID A FILE
      IN A CAKE.
   (C) AN ANGEL OF THE LORD
      GOT HIM OUT.

6. WHAT IS ONE OF THE FOUR LIVING
   CREATURES IN THE VISION OF
   HEAVEN?   REVELATION 4:7
   A. A CAT
   (B) AN EAGLE
   C. A BUDGIE

91

FILL IN THE BLANKS

WORD LIST	
MYSELF	WORK
DESIRED	PLEASED
REWARD	ANY
MISS	WANTED

" ANYTHING I SAW AND
WANTED, I GOT FOR
MYSELF. I DID NOT
MISS ANY
PLEASURE I DESIRED.
I WAS PLEASED WITH
EVERYTHING I DID. AND THIS
PLEASURE WAS THE REWARD
FOR ALL MY HARD WORK."
ECCLESIASTES 2:10

94

TRUE / FALSE

1. LOT WAS THE SON OF ABRAHAM.
   GENESIS 11:31   TRUE ___ FAL

2. SAUL WAS NOT JONATHAN'S
   HE WAS DAVID'S FATHER.
   1 SAMUEL 19:1   TRUE ___ FAL

3. JONATHAN DID NOT LIKE DAVI
   WANTED NOTHING TO DO WITH
   1 SAMUEL 19:2   TRUE ___ FAL

4. SHEM, NOAH'S SON, HAD AN O
   BROTHER NAMED JAPHETH.
   GENESIS 10:21   TRUE ___ FAL

5. MARY WAS PLEDGED, OR BET
   TO MARRY JOSEPH.
   MATTHEW 1:18   TRUE ✓ FAL

89

MULTIPLE CHOICE
CIRCLE THE CORRECT ANSWE

1. WHO WROTE THE BOOK OF EPHE
   IN THE NEW TESTAMENT?
   EPHE
   A. EPHESIA
   B. TIMOTHY
   (C) PAUL

2. HOW MANY LOAVES OF BREAD
   FISH DID JESUS USE TO FEE
   FOUR THOUSAND?
   A. THREE LOAVES OF B
      SEVEN FISH
   (B) SEVEN LOAVES OF B
      A FEW FISH
   C. FOUR THOUSAND LO
      BREAD AND FOUR T
      FISH

3. THE SECOND PLAGUE ON EGYPT
   EXODUS
   (A) FROGS
   B. LOCUSTS
   C. FLIES
   CONT'D NEXT PAGE...

92

FILL IN THE BLANKS

WORD LIST	
WHAT	GAIN
JUST	I
WIND	HARD
CHASING	TIME

" BUT THEN I LOOKED AT
I HAD DONE. I THOUGH
ALL THE HARD WOR
SUDDENLY I REALIZED
JUST A WASTE OF I
LIKE CHASING
THE WIND! THERE
NOTHING TO GAIN F
ANYTHING WE DO HERE
EARTH."
ECCLESIA

95

---

4. HOW DID SAUL KILL HIMSELF?
   1 SAMUEL 31:4
   A. HUNG HIMSELF
   (B) FELL ON A SWORD
   C. ASKED HIS SERVANT TO DO IT

5. HOW DID GOD GUARD THE WAY TO THE
   TREE OF LIFE?   GENESIS 3:24
   A. PUT GATES AROUND IT
   B. MADE IT INVISIBLE
   (C) SENT CHERUBIMS AND A
      FLAMING SWORD

6. HOW DID GOD CREATE THE FIRST
   WOMAN?   GENESIS 2:21-22
   A. OUT OF DUST
   (B) OUT OF ADAM'S RIB
   C. OUT OF ADAM'S
      SHOULDER

93

LL IN THE BLANKS

WORD LIST	
NAL	NOW
ONOR	OBEY
OMMANDS	MOST
EOPLE	HEARD

O W EVERYTHING HAS
EN HEARD. HERE
MY FINAL ADVICE:
ONOR GOD AND
BEY HIS
OMMANDS THIS
THE MOST IMPORTANT
ING PEOPLE CAN
..."

96

FILL IN THE BLANKS

WORD LIST	
EVERYTHING	PLAN
HIS	WORKS
LOVE	PEOPLE
GOD	KNOW

" WE KNOW THAT IN
EVERYTHING
GOD WORKS FOR THE
GOOD OF THOSE WHO LOVE
HIM. THEY ARE THE
PEOPLE GOD
CALLED, BECAUSE THAT WAS
HIS PLAN "

ROMANS 8:28

97

MATCH THE SAYING

MATCH THE SAYING BELOW WITH THE
PERSON WHO SAID IT FROM THE
FOLLOWING PAGE.

1. " I COME AGAINST YOU IN THE NAME OF
   THE LORD ALMIGHTY..."
   DAVID   1 SAMUEL 17:45

2. " MANY WHO HAVE THE HIGHEST PLACE
   NOW WILL HAVE THE LOWEST PLACE
   IN THE FUTURE "
   JESUS   MARK 10:29-31

3. " TO THOSE WHO ARE PURE, ALL
   THINGS ARE PURE, "
   PAUL   TITUS 1:1, 15

4. " COME HERE I'LL FEED YOUR BODY
   TO THE BIRDS OF THE AIR AND THE
   WILD ANIMALS "
   GOLIATH   1 SAMUEL 17:25-44

5. " LOOK! I SEE HEAVEN OPEN, AND I SEE THE
   SON OF MAN STANDING AT GOD'S RIGHT SIDE."
   STEPHEN   ACTS 7:56

98

TCH THE ANSWERS

H THE ANSWERS ON THE FOLLOWING
TO THE QUESTIONS BELOW.

ANOINTED SAUL AS KING OF
AL ?
MUEL   1 SAMUEL 10:1

T'S THE NAME OF THE EIGHTH
K OF THE NEW TESTAMENT ?
ORINTHIANS

RE DOES THE "RIVER OF LIFE"
W FROM ?
ONE OF GOD   REVELATION 22:1

MANY TRUMPETS DID THE
ELS HAVE ?
EVEN   REVELATION 8:6

STREETS OF "NEW JERUSALEM" ARE
E OF WHAT ?
RE GOLD   REVELATION 21:21

O BURIED SAMSON ?
HERS & BROTHERS   JUDGES 16:31

100

ANSWER PAGES

" THEY **TEACH** WISDOM AN
SELF - **CONTROL** . THEY GI
UNDERSTANDING. THEY WILL
TEACH YOU HOW TO BE **WISE**
AND SELF-CONTROLLED. THE
WILL TEACH YOU WHAT IS
HONEST AND FAIR AND
RIGHT . THEY GIVE THE
ABILITY TO **THINK** TO THOS
WITH LITTLE KNOWLEDGE.
THEY GIVE KNOWLEDGE AND
GOOD **SENSE** TO THE YOUN

PROVERBS 1

WORD LIST	
CONTROL	THINK
HONEST	TEACH
SENSE	RIGHT
WISE	YOUNG

100

TRUE / FALSE

1. SAMSON LED THE NATION OF ISRAEL FOR FIFTEEN YEARS.

JUDGES 16:31 TRUE ___ FALSE ✓

2. WHEN THE SOLDIERS SAW THE ANGEL AT THE TOMB OF JESUS, THEY BECAME LIKE DEAD MEN.

MATTHEW 28:2-4 TRUE ✓ FALSE ___

3. THIRD JOHN IS THE TWENTY-FIFTH BOOK IN THE NEW TESTAMENT.

TRUE ✓ FALSE ___

CONT'D NEXT PAGE ...

101

CONT'D FROM PREVIOUS PAGE

4. CORNELIUS' OCCUPATION WAS TENT-MAKING.

ACTS 10:1 TRUE ___ FALSE ✓

5. WE BECOME CHILDREN OF GOD BY PUTTING OUR FAITH IN JESUS CHRIST.

GALATIANS 3:26 TRUE ✓ FALSE ___

6. JOHN THE BAPTIST CALLED HIMSELF A VOICE.

MARK 1:2-3 TRUE ✓ FALSE ___

102

MATCH THE ANSWERS
MATCH THE ANSWERS ON THE FOLLO PAGE TO THE QUESTIONS BELOW

1. WHO ASKED , " WHAT CRIME HAS JES COMMITTED ?"
PILATE MARK 15:14

2. WHO ASKED WHY JESUS ATE WITH T TAX COLLECTORS AND SINNERS ?
PHARISEES MATTHEW 9:

3. WHO SAID , " IT IS NOT THE HEALTH NEED A DOCTOR, BUT THE SICK ?"
JESUS MATTHEW 9

4. WHO SAID , " COME HERE , I'LL FEED BODY TO THE BIRDS OF THE AIR AND WILD ANIMALS ?" ?
GOLIATH 1 SAMUEL 17:

5. WHO ASKED , " AM I MY BROTHER'S KEEPER ?"
CAIN GENESIS

6. WHO ASKED , " WHY HAVEN'T YOU TA CARE OF GOD'S TEMPLE ?"
NEHEMIAH NEHEMIAH 13

103

MULTIPLE CHOICE
CIRCLE THE CORRECT ANSWER .

1. WHICH PROPHET MARRIED AN UNFAITHFUL WIFE NAMED GOMER?
   A. ISAIAH
   Ⓑ HOSEA
   C. JEREMIAH
   (ANSWER FOUND IN VERSE 2-3 OR ONE OF THE ABOVE CHOICES.)

2. WHO WAS ABRAHAM'S SECOND SON?
   Ⓐ ISAAC GENESIS 21:2-3
   B. ISHMAEL
   C. CAIN

3. THE MAGI WERE ...
   A. SOLDIERS MATTHEW 2:11-12
   Ⓑ WISE MEN OR KINGS
   C. SHEPHERDS .

105

CONT'D FROM PREVIOUS PAGE

4. WHAT DOES THE LORD PREPARE IN THE PRESENCE OF OUR ENEMIES? PSALM 23:5
   A. OUR CLOTHES
   B. DINNER
   Ⓒ A TABLE

5. IN THE PARABLE OF THE SOWER , WHERE DID THE SEED FALL THAT WAS CHOKED? MATTHEW 13:7
   A. ON ROCKY SOIL
   Ⓑ AMONG THORNS
   C. AMONG WEEDS

6. WHERE DID LAZARUS, MARTHA, AND MARY LIVE ? JOHN 11:1
   A. JERUSALEM
   Ⓑ BETHANY
   C. NAZARETH

106

FILL IN THE BLANKS

WORD LIST	
LOVED	KINGDOM
BELIEVES	CHILDRE
LIFE	LOVES
BORN	LIKE

1. " FOR GOD **LOVED** THE
WORLD SO MUCH THAT HE G
HIS ONLY SON. GOD GAVE HI
SO THAT WHOEVER **BELIEV**
IN HIM MAY NOT BE LOST B
HAVE ETERNAL **LIFE** . "

2. " I TELL YOU THE TRUTH. UNLE
ONE IS **BORN** AGAIN, HE
NOT BE IN GOD'S **KINGDOM**

3. " YOU ARE GOD'S **CHILDRE**
WHOM HE **LOVES** . SO TR
BE **LIKE** GOD. "

107

FILL IN THE BLANKS

WORD LIST

WORLD	TROUBLES
DEFEATED	HAPPY
HAPPEN	WISDOM
GENEROUS	GIVE

" BROTHERS, YOU WILL HAVE MANY **TROUBLES**, BUT WHEN THESE THINGS **HAPPEN**, YOU SHOULD BE VERY **HAPPY** "
JAMES 1:2

" TOLD YOU THESE THINGS SO THAT YOU CAN HAVE PEACE IN ME. IN THIS **WORLD** YOU WILL HAVE TROUBLE. BUT BE BRAVE ! I HAVE **DEFEATED** THE WORLD ! "
JOHN 16:33

"IF ANY OF YOU NEEDS **WISDOM**, YOU SHOULD ASK GOD FOR IT. GOD IS **GENEROUS**. HE ENJOYS GIVING TO ALL PEOPLE, SO HE WILL **GIVE** YOU WISDOM."
JAMES 1:5

108

FILL IN THE BLANKS

EPHESIANS 6:13-17 IS ABOUT THE ARMOR OF GOD.

THE BELT OF **TRUTH** .

THE BREASTPLATE OF **RIGHTEOUSNESS** .

FEET FITTED WITH **READINESS** .

THE SHIELD OF **FAITH** .

THE HELMET OF **SALVATION** .

THE SWORD OF THE **SPIRIT** .

WORD LIST

TRUTH	RIGHTEOUSNESS
SPIRIT	FAITH
SALVATION	READINESS

111

CON'T'D FROM PREVIOUS PAGE.

5. WHEN ABRAHAM DIED, GOD BLESSED HIS SON, ISAAC
GENESIS 25:11

TRUE **✓** FALSE ___

6. ABRAHAM WAS TESTED BY GOD.
GENESIS 22:1

TRUE **✓** FALSE ___

7. THE QUEEN OF SHEBA CAME TO VISIT SOLOMON SO SHE COULD MARRY HIM.
1 KINGS 10:1-2

TRUE ___ FALSE **✓**

114

MULTIPLE CHOICE

CIRCLE THE CORRECT ANSWER

1. THE SHORTEST CHAPTER IN THE BIBLE IS ...

   A. PHILEMON 1.
   B. PSALM 117.
   C. TITUS 3.

2. WHO WAS CHOSEN TO REPLACE JUDAS ISCARIOT AFTER HE HANGED HIMSELF ?
ACTS 1: 25-26

   A. JAMES
   B. MATTHIAS
   C. ANDREW

3. WHO WAS A " WILD DONKEY OF A MAN " ?
GENESIS 16:11-12

   A. ISAAC
   B. JOHN
   C. ISHMAEL

CON'T'D NEXT PAGE ...

109

WHO WAS HIS MOTHER?

MATCH SON TO MOTHER BY DRAWING A LINE FROM ONE NAME TO ANOTHER.

SOLOMON — RUTH
JOHN 1:12-17

SAMUEL — HAGAR
GENESIS 16:15

OBED — BATHSHEBA
MATTHEW 1:1-6

ISHMAEL — ADAH
GENESIS 36:10

ELIPHAZ — HANNAH
1 SAMUEL 1:20

112

THE TEN COMMANDMENTS

NUMBER THEM SO THEY ARE IN THE RIGHT ORDER.
EXODUS 20: 3-17

12 YOU SHALL NOT MAKE FOR YOURSELVES ANY IDOLS.

9 YOU SHALL NOT LIE AGAINST YOUR NEIGHBOR.

6 YOU MUST NOT MURDER ANYONE.

8 YOU SHALL NOT STEAL.

7 YOU MUST NOT BE GUILTY OF ADULTERY.

CON'T'D NEXT PAGE ...

115

CON'T'D FROM PREVIOUS PAGE.

4. WHAT EVANGELIST HAD FOUR DAUGHTERS WHO PROPHESIED ?
ACTS 21:8-9

   A. ABRAHAM
   B. PHILIP
   C. ZACCHAEUS

5. AT WHAT HOUR OF THE DAY DID JESUS DIE!
ACTS 11: 24-27

   A. THE THIRD HOUR
   B. THE NINTH HOUR
   C. THE SIXTH HOUR

6. HOW TALL WAS GOLIATH ?
1 SAMUEL 17:4

   A. OVER EIGHT FEET
   B. OVER NINE FEET
   C. OVER TEN FEET

110

TRUE / FALSE

1. MATTHIAS REPLACED PETER AS AN APOSTLE.
ACTS 1: 24-26

TRUE ___ FALSE **✓**

2. PHILIP BAPTIZED AN ETHIOPIAN EUNUCH.
ACTS 8:38

TRUE **✓** FALSE ___

3. THE DEATH OF THE FIRSTBORN WAS ONE OF THE PLAGUES OF EGYPT.
EXODUS 12: 4-6

TRUE **✓** FALSE ___

4. JESUS SAID A PROPHET HAS HONOR IN HIS OWN TOWN.
MATTHEW 13:57-58

TRUE ___ FALSE **✓**

CON'T'D NEXT PAGE ...

113

CON'T'D FROM PREVIOUS PAGE.

10 YOU SHALL NOT COVET ANYTHING BELONGING TO YOUR NEIGHBOR.

1 YOU SHALL HAVE NO OTHER GODS BEFORE ME.

3 YOU MUST NOT USE THE NAME OF THE LORD YOUR GOD THOUGHTLESSLY.

4 REMEMBER THE SABBATH BY KEEPING IT HOLY.

5 HONOR YOUR FATHER AND MOTHER.

116

FILL IN THE BLANKS

WORD LIST	
LOVE	SOUL
NEIGHBOR	HEART
LORD	MIND
GOD	YOURSELF

" _LOVE_ THE _LORD_ YOUR
GOD WITH ALL YOUR _HEART_
AND WITH ALL YOUR _SOUL_
AND WITH ALL YOUR _MIND_ . "

Matthew 22:37

" LOVE YOUR _NEIGHBOR_ AS
YOU LOVE _YOURSELF_ . "

Matthew 22:39

117

FILL IN THE BLANKS

WORD LIST	
ADVICE	CHAIN
TEACHING	FATHER'S
LISTEN	MOTHER'S
FLOWERS	LIFE

" MY CHILD, _LISTEN_ TO YOUR
FATHER'S _TEACHING_ AND
DO NOT FORGET YOUR _MOTHER'S_
ADVICE . "

" THEIR TEACHING WILL BEAUTIFY
YOUR _LIFE_ IT WILL BE LIKE
FLOWERS IN YOUR HAIR OR
A _CHAIN_ AROUND YOUR
NECK. "

PROVERBS 1:8,9

118

MATCH THE ANSWER

MATCH THE ANSWERS ON THE FOLL
PAGE TO THIS QUESTIONS BELO

1. WHERE WAS RUTH'S HOMELA
   MOAB
   Ruth 1

2. WHO WAS THE THIRD SON OF
   SETH

3. WHERE WAS JACOB BURIED
   CANAAN

4. WHO SAID, " IF ANYONE IS NOT
   ME, THEN HE IS AGAINST ME "
   JESUS
   Matthew

5. WHO WAS HOSEA'S FATHER ?
   BEERI

6. IN THE GOSPEL OF JOHN, WHO
   JESUS WEEP FOR ?
   LAZARUS
   John 11:

119

MATCH THE ANSWERS

MATCH THE ANSWERS ON THE FOLLOWING
PAGE TO THE QUESTIONS BELOW.

1. WHO WAS THE FIRST CHRISTIAN
   MARTYR ?
   STEPHEN
   Acts 7:59-60

2. WHAT TWELVE-YEAR-OLD GIRL WAS
   BROUGHT BACK TO LIFE BY JESUS ?
   JAIRUS' DAUGHTER
   Luke 8:49-56

3. WHO GAVE MOSES HIS NAME ?
   PHARAOH'S DAUGHTER
   Exodus 2:10

4. WHO TOLD NOAH TO COME OUT OF
   THE ARK ?
   GOD
   Genesis 8:15-16

5. IN WHAT TOWN WAS JETHRO A
   PRIEST ?
   MIDIAN
   Exodus 18:1

6. WHAT WAS THE NAME OF THE
   CENTURION PAUL WAS HANDED OVER
   TO ?
   JULIUS
   Acts 27:1

121

MULTIPLE CHOICE

CIRCLE THE CORRECT ANSWER.

1. WHAT HAPPENED WHEN PHARAOH
   WOULD NOT LET MOSES AND HIS
   PEOPLE GO !
   Exodus 12:29
   (A) EVERY FIRSTBORN DIED.
   B. EVERY SECONDBORN DIED.
   C. THE RIVER DRIED UP.

2. TO WHAT DID PAUL COMPARE THE
   COMING OF " THE DAY OF THE LORD " ?
   1 Thessalonians 5:2
   A. A ROAR OF THUNDER
   B. A FLASH OF LIGHTNING
   (C) A THIEF IN THE NIGHT

3. WHAT HAPPENED TO PETER WHEN JESUS
   ASKED HIM TO WALK ON WATER ?
   Matthew 14:30-31
   A. HE DROWNED.
   (B) HE SANK FOR LACK OF FAITH.
   C. AN ANGEL CARRIED HIM.

CONT'D NEXT PAGE ...

123

CONT'D FROM PREVIOUS PAGE

4. WHO WAS BLINDED BY JESUS ON THE
   WAY TO DAMASCUS ?
   Acts 9:8
   (A) PAUL
   B. SAUL
   C. PETER

5. WHO DID THE LORD CALL BY A VISION
   IN DAMASCUS ?
   Acts 9:10
   (A) ANANIAS
   B. PETER
   C. PAUL

6. WHAT DID THE ANGEL MEASURE
   THE CITY WITH ?
   Revelation 21:16
   A. A MEASURING TAPE
   B. A STICK
   (C) A SQUARE AS LONG AS
   WIDE AND HIGH

124

FILL IN THE BLANKS

WORD LIST	
SAY	UNDERSTANDING
COMMAND	WISDOM
LISTEN	HEART
REMEMBER	CHILD

" MY _CHILD_ , BELIEVE WHAT
I _SAY_ AND _REMEMBER_
WHAT I _COMMAND_ YOU.
LISTEN TO _WISDOM_ TRY
WITH ALL YOUR _HEART_ TO
GAIN _UNDERSTANDING_ "

PROVERBS 2:1,2

125

FILL IN THE BLANKS

WORD LIST	
HIM	KNOWLEDGE
LORD	INNOCENT
HONEST	PROTECTS
WISDOM	SHIELD

" ONLY THE _LORD_ GIVES
WISDOM _KNOWLEDGE_ AND
UNDERSTANDING COME FROM
HIM . HE STORES UP WISDOM
FOR THOSE WHO ARE _INNOCENT_ .
LIKE A _SHIELD_ HE
PROTECTS THOSE WHO ARE
HONEST "

PROVERBS 2:6,7

126

MULTIPLE CHOICE

CIRCLE THE CORRECT ANSWER.

1. WHAT WAS THE FIRST TREE MENTIONED
   IN THE BIBLE ?
   Genesis 2:9
   A. APPLE
   B. CEDAR
   (C) TREE OF LIFE

2. HOW OLD WAS JOSHUA WHEN HE
   DIED ?
   Joshua 24:29
   (A) ONE HUNDRED AND TEN
   B. ONE HUNDRED AND TWELVE
   C. SIXTY-SEVEN

3. WHO WAS MARY'S FATHER-IN-LAW ?
   Matthew 1:16
   A. DAVID
   B. ZECHARIAH
   (C) JACOB

CONT'D NEXT PAGE ...

127

'D FROM PREVIOUS PAGE

WHOSE BONES WERE CARRIED FORTY YEARS THROUGH THE DESERT? *JOSHUA 24:32*

A. MOSES'
B. JOSEPH'S
C. ADAM'S

WHAT DID JAMES SAY MAN COULD NOT TAME? *JAMES 3:8*

A. A BEAR
B. A LION
C. THE TONGUE

HOW LONG WAS JONAH IN THE BELLY OF THE FISH? *JONAH 1:17*

A. THREE DAYS AND NIGHTS
B. SEVEN DAYS AND NIGHTS
C. THIRTY DAYS AND NIGHTS

128

MULTIPLE CHOICE
CIRCLE THE CORRECT ANSWER

1. WHY DID MOSES BREAK THE TABLETS OF THE TEN COMMANDMENTS? *EXODUS 32:19*

   A. THEY WERE TOO HEAVY.
   B. HE DROPPED THEM.
   C. HE WAS ANGRY AT THE ISRAELITES.

2. WHAT WAS THE SIGN OF THE PROMISE BETWEEN GOD AND NOAH? *GENESIS 9:12-13*

   A. A RAINBOW
   B. THE RAIN
   C. THE ARK

3. WHAT DOES THE NAME "EVE" MEAN? *GENESIS 3:20*

   A. MOTHER OF EVENING
   B. MOTHER OF ALL LIVING
   C. BEGINNING OF NIGHT

CONT'D NEXT PAGE...

129

CONT'D FROM PREVIOUS PAGE

4. WHAT IS THE FOURTEENTH BOOK OF THE OLD TESTAMENT?

   A. SECOND CHRONICLES
   B. FIRST CHRONICLES
   C. SECOND KINGS

5. WHAT HAPPENED TO THE YOUTH THAT MADE FUN OF ELISHA'S BALDNESS? *2 KINGS 2:23-24*

   A. THEY WERE SENT TO THEIR ROOMS.
   B. THEY WERE MAULED BY BEARS.
   C. THEY HAD TO APOLOGIZE.

6. HOW OLD WAS JEHORAM WHEN HE BECAME KING OF JUDAH? *2 CHRONICLES 21:5*

   A. TWELVE
   B. THIRTY-TWO
   C. TWENTY-FIVE

130

UNSCRAMBLE THE VERSE
TO FIND OUT WHAT THE VERSE BELOW FILL IN THE BLANKS. ALL THE VOWELS ARE THERE. ALL YOU NEED TO DO IS ADD THE CONSONANTS.

"... CHILD, OD TNO TFEORG YM ... AHC. NTHE UOV IWLL ... A GNLO MTEI. DNA RYUO LILW EB SLSUUFCECE."

"_CHILD, DO NOT_
FORGET MY
TEACHING ...
THEN YOU WILL
LIVE A LONG
TIME. AND
YOUR LIFE WILL
_SUCCESSFUL."

PROVERBS 3:1-2

131

UNSCRAMBLE THE VERSE
TO FIND OUT WHAT THE VERSE BELOW SAYS, FILL IN THE BLANKS. ALL THE VOWELS ARE THERE. ALL YOU NEED TO DO IS ADD THE CONSONANTS.

"TTSUR HET DLRO TWHI LAL
RUVO TLARE. OTON DNDEPE
NO RYUO NOW OREUNSINDTAG
KREMMEBE ETH DLOR NI
EEVYRGHINT UVO OD. DNA EH
LLWI EIGV YUO SSSCCEU."

"_TRUST THE LORD_
WITH ALL YOUR
HEART. DON'T
DEPEND ON YOUR
OWN UNDER-
STANDING.
REMEMBER THE
LORD IN EVERYTHING
YOU DO. AND HE WILL
_GIVE YOU SUCCESS."

PROVERBS 3:5-6

132

TRUE / FALSE

1. MARY, JESUS' MOTHER, WAS NOT AT THE CRUCIFIXION. *JOHN 19:25*

   TRUE ___ FALSE ✓

2. JESUS HAD NO BROTHERS OR SISTERS. *MARK 6:3*

   TRUE ___ FALSE ✓

3. ISAIAH WAS AN APOSTLE. *2 CHRONICLES 32:20*

   TRUE ___ FALSE ✓

CONT'D NEXT PAGE...

133

'D FROM PREVIOUS PAGE

JESUS WAS TWELVE YEARS OLD WHEN HE FIRST SPOKE AT THE TEMPLE. *LUKE 2:42-46*

TRUE ___ FALSE ✓

BARNABAS WAS A FOLLOWER OF JESUS. *ACTS 11:22-24*

TRUE ✓ FALSE ___

KING DAVID MOVED THE ARK OF THE COVENANT FROM THE HOUSE OF ABINADAB TO THE TABERNACLE. *2 SAMUEL 6:1-17*

TRUE ✓ FALSE ___

134

TRUE / FALSE

1. SOLOMON WAS DAVID'S SON. *1 KINGS 2:1*

   TRUE ✓ FALSE ___

2. DAVID KILLED SIX HUNDRED OF THE ARAMEAN CHARIOTEERS AND THIRTY THOUSAND OF THEIR FOOT SOLDIERS. *2 SAMUEL 10:18*

   TRUE ___ FALSE ✓

3. ABRAHAM WAS TESTED BY GOD. *GENESIS 22:1*

   TRUE ✓ FALSE ___

CONT'D NEXT PAGE...

135

CONT'D FROM PREVIOUS PAGE

4. GOD DESTROYED SODOM AND GOMORRAH. *GENESIS 19:24*

   TRUE ✓ FALSE ___

5. SIMON THE SORCERER BECAME A FOLLOWER OF JESUS CHRIST. *ACTS 8:13*

   TRUE ✓ FALSE ___

6. ELISABETH, WIFE OF ZACHARIAS, WAS A DESCENDANT OF AARON. *LUKE 1:5*

   TRUE ✓ FALSE ___

136

MATCH THE ANSWERS

MATCH THE ANSWERS ON THE FOLLOWING PAGE TO THE QUESTIONS BELOW.

1. WHAT DID EZEKIEL EAT THAT WAS AS SWEET AS HONEY?
THE SCROLL *EZEKIEL 3:3*

2. WHO WAS TOLD IN A VISION ABOUT HIS SON'S BIRTH?
ZACHARIAS *LUKE 1:11-13*

3. IN WHAT PROVINCE DID JESUS MEET THE FISHERMEN?
GALILEE *MATTHEW 4:18-19*

4. WHERE WAS JACOB BURIED?
EGYPT *GENESIS 50:13-14*

5. WHO WAS SOLOMON'S MOTHER?
BATHSHEBA *1 KINGS 1:11*

6. WHAT IS THE LAST WORD IN THE BIBLE?
AMEN *REVELATION 22:21*

137

CONT'D FROM PREVIOUS PAGE.

4. THE NAME "ABRAHAM" MEANS ...? *GENESIS 17:5*
- **A. FATHER OF NATIONS**
- B. FATHER OF ISAAC
- C. FATHER OF ALL

5. HOW MANY DAYS DID WATER FLOOD THE EARTH? *GENESIS 7:24*
- A. SEVEN DAYS
- B. THIRTY DAYS
- **C. ONE HUNDRED AND FIFTY DAYS**

HOW MANY PEOPLE WERE KILLED WHEN SAMSON DESTROYED THE TEMPLE OF DAGON? *JUDGES 16:27-30*
- **A. THREE THOUSAND**
- B. THIRTY THOUSAND
- C. THREE HUNDRED THOUSAND

142

FINISH THE VERSE

TO FIND OUT WHAT THE VERSE BELOW SAYS, FILL IN THE BLANKS. ALL THE CONSONANTS ARE THERE. ALL YOU NEED TO DO IS ADD THE VOWELS.

VOWELS: A E I O U

"DON'T DEPEND ON YOUR OWN WISDOM. RESPECT THE LORD AND REFUSE TO DO WRONG. THEN YOUR BODY WILL BE HEALTHY AND YOUR BONES WILL BE STRONG."

PROVERBS 3:7-8

145

MATCH THE ANSWERS

MATCH THE ANSWERS ON THE FOLLOWING PAGE TO THE QUESTIONS BELOW.

1. WHERE WAS JESUS BORN? *LUKE 2:4-6*
BETHLEHEM

2. WHAT BABY WAS FOUND IN A BASKET IN A RIVER? *EXODUS 2:3-10*
MOSES

3. WHAT WAS THE THIRD PLAGUE THE LORD BROUGHT ON PHARAOH? *EXODUS 8:16-17*
PLAGUE OF LICE

4. WHO WAS AARON'S SISTER? *EXODUS 15:20*
MIRIAM

5. IN WHAT CITY WAS RAHAB AND THOSE IN HER HOUSE THE ONLY SURVIVORS? *JOSHUA 6:17-25*
JERICHO

6. IN WHAT MONTH DID THE ARK COME TO REST ON MOUNT ARARAT? *GENESIS 8:4*
SEVENTH MONTH

139

MULTIPLE CHOICE

CIRCLE THE CORRECT ANSWER.

1. WHAT HAPPENED TO PHARAOH'S ARMY WHEN THEY CHASED AFTER MOSES AND HIS PEOPLE? *EXODUS 14:26-28*
- A. THEY GOT SAND IN THEIR EYES.
- B. THEY GOT TIRED OF THE CHASE.
- **C. THEY DROWNED IN THE RED SEA.**

2. WHAT DID ELIJAH CALL DOWN FROM HEAVEN? *1 KINGS 1:10-12*
- **A. FIRE**
- B. RAIN
- C. ANGELS

3. HOW DID JUDAS IDENTIFY JESUS FOR THE SOLDIERS? *MATTHEW 26:48-49*
- A. BY POINTING HIM OUT
- **B. WITH A KISS**
- C. BY A HAND ON HIS SHOULDER

CONT'D NEXT PAGE ...

143

FINISH THE VERSE

TO FIND OUT WHAT THE VERSE BELOW SAYS, FILL IN THE BLANKS. ALL THE CONSONANTS ARE THERE. ALL YOU NEED TO DO IS ADD THE VOWELS.

VOWELS: A E I O U

"MY CHILD, DO NOT REJECT THE LORD'S DISCIPLINE AND DON'T BE ANGRY WHEN HE CORRECTS YOU. THE LORD CORRECTS THOSE HE LOVES, JUST AS A FATHER CORRECTS THE CHILD THAT HE LOVES."

PROVERBS 3:11-12

146

MULTIPLE CHOICE

CIRCLE THE CORRECT ANSWER.

1. HOW MANY CHARIOTS AND HORSES DID SOLOMON HAVE? *1 KINGS 10:26*
- **A. FOURTEEN HUNDRED CHARIOTS, TWELVE THOUSAND HORSES**
- B. TWELVE THOUSAND CHARIOTS, FOURTEEN THOUSAND HORSES
- C. TWELVE THOUSAND CHARIOTS, FOURTEEN HUNDRED HORSES

2. WHERE DID ADAM AND EVE FIRST LIVE? *GENESIS 2:15*
- A. BABYLON
- **B. GARDEN OF EDEN**
- C. ISRAEL

3. WHAT DID PAUL HAVE IN TROAS? *ACTS 16:9*
- A. A COLD
- B. A DREAM
- **C. A VISION**

CONT'D NEXT PAGE ...

141

CONT'D FROM PREVIOUS PAGE.

4. WHAT LESSON DID JESUS TEACH HIS DISCIPLES BY WASHING THEIR FEET? *JOHN 13*
- A. TO KEEP THEIR FEET CLEAN
- **B. TO SERVE OTHERS**
- C. ABOUT CEREMONIAL CLEANSING

5. WHAT DID GOD CREATE TO SEPARATE DAY FROM LIGHT? *GENESIS 1*
- A. FIRE
- **B. LIGHTS (STARS) IN THE SKY**
- C. ELECTRIC LIGHTS

6. FINISH PAUL'S SENTENCE " ALL PEOPLE HAVE SINNED AND ..." *ROMANS 3*
- **A. ARE NOT GOOD ENOUGH FOR GOD**
- B. SHOULD BE PUNISHED
- C. NEED FORGIVENESS

144

TRUE / FALSE

1. THE LORD CREATED THE GARDEN OF EDEN. *GENESIS 2:8*
TRUE ___ FALSE **✓**

2. IT WAS IN THE CITY OF LUZ (OR BETHEL) WHERE JACOB HAD HIS DREAM ON THE LADDER. *GENESIS 28:19*
TRUE **✓** FALSE ___

3. LOT PLEADED WITH THE LORD TO SAVE SODOM. *GENESIS 18:16*
TRUE ___ FALSE ___

CONT'D NEXT PAGE ...

147

CON'D FROM PREVIOUS PAGE.

ADAM PERSUADED EVE TO EAT FROM THE TREE OF THE KNOWLEDGE OF GOOD AND EVIL.

GENESIS 3:6

TRUE ___ FALSE ✓

A RIVER FLOWED OUT OF THE GARDEN OF EDEN.

GENESIS 2:10

TRUE ✓ FALSE ___

GOD CREATED ALL OTHER LIVING CREATURES BEFORE HE CREATED MAN.

GENESIS 1:20-26

TRUE ✓ FALSE ___

148

TRUE / FALSE

1. TROPHIMUS WAS THOUGHT TO HAVE BEEN BROUGHT INTO THE TEMPLE WITH PAUL.

ACTS 21:26-29

TRUE ✓ FALSE ___

2. TROPHIMUS WAS AN EGYPTIAN.

ACTS 21:29

TRUE ___ FALSE ✓

3. JETHRO WAS MOSES' SON-IN-LAW.

EXODUS 18:12

TRUE ___ FALSE ✓

CON'D NEXT PAGE ...

149

CON'D FROM PREVIOUS PAGE.

4. AFTER JESUS HAD FASTED IN THE WILDERNESS, ANGELS MINISTERED TO HIM.

MATTHEW 4:11

TRUE ✓ FALSE ___

5. THE LAKE OF FIRE IS THE SECOND DEATH IN THE BOOK OF REVELATION.

REVELATION 20:14

TRUE ✓ FALSE ___

6. PAUL DID NOT VISIT ICONIUM TO PREACH THE GOSPEL.

ACTS 13:51-14:1

TRUE ___ FALSE ✓

150

MATCH THE ANSWERS

MATCH THE ANSWERS ON THE FOLLOWING PAGE TO THE QUESTIONS BELOW.

WHO ROLLED BACK THE STONE FROM JESUS' TOMB?

AN ANGEL OF THE LORD

MATTHEW 28:2

WHAT CITY THAT PAUL VISITED HAD HERE A SIGN THAT READ, "TO A GOD WHO IS NOT KNOWN"?

ATHENS

WHO HAD A VISION OF A GREAT THRONE SURROUNDED BY TWENTY-FOUR ELDERS?

JOHN

REVELATION 4:1-4

WHAT WAS URIAH'S OCCUPATION?

SOLDIER

2 SAMUEL 11:16-17

WHO WAS THE MOTHER OF KING JOASH?

ZIBIAH

2 CHRONICLES 24:1

HOW MANY WIVES DID KING JOASH HAVE?

TWO

2 CHRONICLES 24:3

151

MATCH THE ANSWERS

MATCH THE ANSWERS ON THIS FOLLOWING PAGE TO THE QUESTIONS BELOW.

1. WHO SAID, "LOOK! I SEE HEAVEN OPEN AND I SEE THE SON OF MAN STANDING AT GOD'S RIGHT SIDE"?

STEPHEN

ACTS 7:55-56

2. WHO SANG, "GOD FILLS THE HUNGRY WITH GOOD THINGS, BUT HE SENDS THE RICH AWAY WITH NOTHING"?

MARY

LUKE 1:46-53

3. WHO CALLED HIS FOLLOWERS "THE SALT OF THE EARTH"?

JESUS

MATTHEW 5:13

4. IN WHAT LAND WAS PAUL FORBIDDEN TO PREACH BY THE HOLY SPIRIT?

PHILIPPI

ACTS 16:6

5. WHAT KIND OF SNAKE BIT THE APOSTLE PAUL?

VIPER

ACTS 28:3

6. HOW OLD WAS ISAAC WHEN JACOB AND ESAU WERE BORN?

SIXTY

GENESIS 25:26

153

MULTIPLE CHOICE

CIRCLE THE CORRECT ANSWER

1. DANIEL WAS A...?

MATTHEW 24:15

(A) PROPHET.

B. DISCIPLE.

C. APOSTLE.

2. WHO WAS MELCHIZEDEK?

HEBREWS 7:1-3
GENESIS 14:18

A. A PROPHET

B. A PHARISEE

(C) A HIGH PRIEST

3. WHO IS BEELZEBUB?

MATTHEW 12:24-27

(A) SATAN

B. A PROPHET

C. A KING

CON'D NEXT PAGE ...

155

MULTIPLE CHOICE

CIRCLE THE CORRECT ANSWER.

1. WHEN THE ISRAELITES SPOKE OUT AGAINST GOD AND MOSES IN THE DESERT, WHAT DID GOD SEND THEM?

NUMBERS 21:46

(A) POISONOUS SNAKES

B. QUAIL

C. MANNA

2. WHAT BROTHERS WERE GIVEN THE NAME, "SONS OF THUNDER"?

MARK 3:17

(A) JOHN AND JAMES

B. CAIN AND ABEL

C. PEREZ AND ZERAH

3. JESUS TAUGHT IN PARABLES; WHAT IS A PARABLE?

A. A BOOK OF MANY STORIES

B. A RIDDLE

(C) A WAY OF TEACHING BY COMPARING THINGS TO GET THE MEANING

CON'D NEXT PAGE ...

157

CON'D FROM PREVIOUS PAGE

4. THE NAME "ISAAC" MEANS...?

GENESIS 17:17
18:12-15

(A) ONE WHO LAUGHS

B. STRONG AND MIGHTY

C. GRATITUDE.

5. WHAT DOES THE NAME "ESAU" MEAN?

GENESIS 25:25

A. BALD

(B) HAIRY

C. SLIM

6. WHAT TEMPLE DID SAMSON TEAR DOWN WHEN HE REGAINED HIS STRENGTH?

JUDGES 16:23-30

(A) TEMPLE OF DAGON

B. SYNAGOGUE

C. ZERUBBABEL'S TEMPLE

158

CON'D FROM PREVIOUS PAGE

HOW MANY BOOKS ARE IN THE NEW TESTAMENT?

A. TWENTY

(B) TWENTY-SEVEN

C. TWENTY-EIGHT

WHO WAS HOSEA'S FIRST SON?

HOSEA 1:3-4

(A) JEZREEL

B. SIMON

C. HOSEA, JR.

WHAT DID MOSES DO TO GET WATER OUT OF THE ROCK?

EXODUS 17:5-6

A. HIT IT WITH A HAMMER

(B) STRUCK IT WITH HIS STAFF

C. KICKED IT

156

MATCH THE PARABLE

MATCH THE SCRIPTURE REFERENCE ON THIS FOLLOWING PAGE TO THE PARABLE BELOW!

1. THE WISE AND FOOLISH BUILDERS.
   MATTHEW 7:24-27

2. THE MUSTARD SEED.
   MARK 4:30-32

3. THE PEARL OF GREAT PRICE.
   MATTHEW 13:45-46

4. THE LOST SHEEP.
   LUKE 15:3-7

5. THE PRODIGAL SON.
   LUKE 15:11-32

6. THE WEDDING BANQUET.
   MATTHEW 22:1-14

7. THE GOOD SAMARITAN.
   LUKE 10:30-37

8. THE UNMERCIFUL SERVANT.
   MATTHEW 18:23-35

159

FILL IN THE BLANKS

WORD LIST
WISDOM	SIGHT
OUT	REASON
LIFE	CHILD
NECKLACE	YOUR

" MY _CHILD_ , HOLD ON TO _WISDOM_ AND _REASON_ . DON'T LET THEM _OUT_ OF YOUR _SIGHT_ . THEY WILL GIVE YOU _LIFE_ . LIKE A _NECKLACE_ , THEY WILL BEAUTIFY _YOUR_ LIFE . "

PROVERBS 3:21-22

160

FILL IN THE BLANK

WORD LIST
PEACEFUL	DOWN
NEED	AFRAID
SLEEP	HURT
SAFETY	LIE

" THEN YOU WILL GO ON YOUR WAY IN _SAFETY_ . AND YOU WILL NOT GET _HURT_ . YOU WON'T _NEED_ TO BE _AFRAID_ WHEN YOU LIE _DOWN_ . WHEN YOU LIE DOWN, YOUR _SLEEP_ WILL BE _PEACEFUL_ . "

PROVERBS

161

FILL IN THE BLANKS

WORD LIST
KEEP	LORD
PEOPLE	GOOD
HELP	SAFE
TRAPPED	ABLE

" THE _LORD_ WILL KEEP YOU _SAFE_ . HE WILL _KEEP_ YOU FROM BEING _TRAPPED_ . WHENEVER YOU ARE _ABLE_ , DO _GOOD_ TO _PEOPLE_ WHO NEED _HELP_ . "

PROVERBS 3:26-27

162

FILL IN THE BLANKS

WORD LIST
TEACH	GOOD
UNDERSTAND	TELLING
ATTENTION	TEACHING
FORGET	CHILDREN

" MY _CHILDREN_ , LISTEN TO YOUR FATHER'S _TEACHING_ . PAY _ATTENTION_ SO YOU WILL _UNDERSTAND_ WHAT I AM _TELLING_ YOU IS _GOOD_ . DO NOT _FORGET_ WHAT I _TEACH_ YOU . "

PROVERBS 4:1-2

163

MULTIPLE CHOICE

CIRCLE THE CORRECT ANSWER

1. RIGHT AFTER JESUS WAS BAPTIZED A VOICE FROM HEAVEN SAID WHAT?

   A. "THIS IS MY SON AND I LOVE HIM. I AM VERY PLEASED WITH HIM."

   B. " THIS IS MY SON AND HE IS THE WAY TO HEAVEN."

   C. "THIS IS MY SON, FOLLOW HIM."

2. WHO ASKED JESUS WHETHER IT WAS RIGHT TO PAY TAXES TO THE ROMANS?
   MATTHEW 22

   A. HIS PARENTS

   B. HIS DISCIPLES

   C. THE PHARISEES

3. HOW OLD WAS ENOCH WHEN THE LORD TOOK HIM?
   GENESIS

   A. SIXTY FIVE YEARS

   B. THREE HUNDRED AND SIXTY-FIVE YEARS

   C. SEVENTY YEARS OLD

CONT'D NEXT PAGE...

164

CONT'D FROM PREVIOUS PAGE.

4. IN WHAT CITY WAS PAUL ALMOST WHIPPED FOR SPEAKING TO THE PEOPLE?
   ACTS 22:22-29

   A. ROME

   B. JERUSALEM

   C. MACEDONIA

5. HOW MANY YEARS DID GOD ADD TO KING HEZEKIAH'S LIFE?
   ISAIAH 38:5

   A. FIVE

   B. TEN

   C. FIFTEEN

6. HOW MANY YEARS DID THE ISRAELITES LIVE IN EGYPT?
   EXODUS 12:40-41

   A. FOUR HUNDRED YEARS

   B. FOUR HUNDRED AND THIRTY YEARS

   C. FIVE HUNDRED YEARS

165

MULTIPLE CHOICE

CIRCLE THE CORRECT ANSWER

1. WHERE DID MOSES GO AFTER KILLING THE EGYPTIAN?
   EXODUS 2:15

   A. HOME

   B. JUDAH

   C. MIDIAN

2. MOSES WAS WATCHING A FLOCK OF SHEEP WHEN THE LORD CAME TO HIM. WHOSE FLOCK WAS HE WATCHING?
   EXODUS 3:1

   A. THE KING'S

   B. HIS FATHER'S

   C. JETHRO'S

3. IN WHAT MONTH DID THE ANGEL APPEAR TO THE VIRGIN MARY?
   LUKE 1:26-27

   A. THIRD MONTH

   B. SIXTH MONTH

   C. NINTH MONTH

CONT'D NEXT PAGE ...

166

CONT'D FROM PREVIOUS PAGE.

4. WHO MADE HIS WIFE PASS AS HIS SISTER?
   GENESIS 20:2

   A. MOSES

   B. ABRAHAM

   C. ISAAC

5. WHAT WAS THE POTTER'S FIELD KNOWN AS?
   MATTHEW 27

   A. FIELD OF BLOOD

   B. FIELD OF POTTERS

   C. FIELD OF DEATH

6. WHO TURNED HIS STAFF INTO A SNAKE?
   EXODUS 7:10

   A. MOSES

   B. AARON

   C. PAUL

167

[M]ATCH THE ANSWERS

MATCH THE ANSWERS ON THE FOLLOWING
[PA]GE TO THE QUESTIONS BELOW.

[WH]O WAS EPHRAIM'S FATHER ?
JOSEPH *Genesis 41:50-52*

[WHA]T WAS HEZEKIAH'S
[OCC]UPATION ?
[K]ING *2 Chronicles 29:1*

[WH]O WAS THE LAST PROPHET OF THE
[OLD] TESTAMENT ?
MALACHI

[ON WHI]CH MOUNTAIN DID MOSES
[RE]CEIVE THE TEN COMMANDMENTS ?
[M]OUNT SINAI *Exodus 19:20-20:17*

[WH]ERE DID NOAH'S ARK COME
[TO] REST ?
[M]OUNTAINS OF ARARAT *Genesis 8:4*

[W]HO PLAYED A MADMAN TO ESCAPE
[F]ROM HIS ENEMIES ?
DAVID *1 Samuel 21:12-15*

168

[CONT'D FROM PREVIOUS PAGE]

BARSABAS WAS AN APOSTLE.
Acts 1:23-26
TRUE ____ FALSE ✓

ABRAHAM LEFT EVERYTHING TO HIS
SON ISAAC WHEN HE DIED.
Genesis 25:5
TRUE ✓ FALSE ____

BECAUSE ESAU WANTED TO KILL
JACOB, JACOB FLED TO HARAN.
Genesis 27:41-43
TRUE ✓ FALSE ____

173

WHO SAID ?

MATCH THE NAMES ON THE FOLLOWING
PAGE TO THE SAYINGS BELOW.

" BUT IF A MAN IS ALREADY OLD, HOW
CAN HE BE BORN AGAIN ? "
NICODEMUS *John 3:4*

" I AM NOT GUILTY OF THIS MAN'S
DEATH. YOU ARE THE ONES CAUSING
IT. "
PONTIUS PILATE *Matthew 27:24*

" YOU WILL NOT DIE. "
THE SERPENT *Genesis 3:4*

" TEACHER, I WANT TO SEE. "
BARTIMAEUS *Mark 10:46-52*

" HE MUST BECOME GREATER AND I
MUST BECOME LESS IMPORTANT. "
JOHN THE BAPTIST *John 3:25-30*

" NO! YOU WILL NEVER WASH MY
FEET ! "
PETER *John 13:8*

176

MATCH THE ANSWERS

MATCH THE ANSWERS ON THE FOLLOWING
PAGE TO THE QUESTIONS BELOW.

1. HOW MANY JARS OF WATER DID
JESUS CHANGE TO WINE?
SIX JARS *John 2:1-10*

2. WHAT OBJECT BROUGHT JOSEPH'S
BROTHERS BACK TO EGYPT ?
A SILVER CUP *Genesis 44:1-13*

3. HOW MANY BOOKS OF THE BIBLE DID
JESUS WRITE ?
NONE

4. AT WHAT AGE DID LAMECH DIE ?
**SEVEN HUNDRED
AND SEVENTY-SEVEN** *Genesis 5:31*

5. WHO WAS LAMECH'S FATHER ?
METHUSELAH *Genesis 5:25*

6. WHAT PROPHET WAS COMMANDED BY
GOD TO GO TO NINEVEH ?
JONAH *Jonah 1:1-2*

170

TRUE / FALSE

1. IT TOOK ELISHA JUST ONE TRY TO SET
FIRE TO HIS WATER-DRENCHED
SACRIFICE.
1 Kings 18:36-38
TRUE ____ FALSE ✓

2. SOLOMON WAS MADE KING BEFORE
DAVID DIED.
1 Kings 1:43-48
TRUE ✓ FALSE ____

3. AARON DIED ON MOUNT HOR AFTER
MOSES GAVE HIS PRIESTLY CLOTHES TO HIS
SON.
Numbers 20:27-28
TRUE ✓ FALSE ____

CONT'D NEXT PAGE ...

174

WHO SAID ?

MATCH THE NAMES ON THE FOLLOWING
PAGE TO THE SAYINGS BELOW.

1. " I WILL GIVE HALF OF MY MONEY TO THE
POOR. IF I HAVE CHEATED ANYONE, I
WILL PAY THAT PERSON BACK FOUR
TIMES MORE ! "
ZACCHAEUS *Luke 19:8*

2. " A MAN HAS TOLD ME EVERYTHING I HAVE
EVER DONE. COME SEE HIM. MAYBE HE IS
THE CHRIST. "
THE SAMARITAN WOMAN *John 4:5-29*

3. " I HAVE SINNED AGAINST THE LORD. "
DAVID *2 Samuel 12:13*

4. " I SINNED. I GAVE YOU AN INNOCENT
MAN TO KILL. "
JUDAS ISCARIOT *Matthew 27:3-4*

5. " COME FOLLOW ME. I WILL MAKE YOU
FISHERMEN FOR ME. "
JESUS *Matthew 4:18-19*

6. " BUT MAYBE YOU DON'T WANT TO SERVE
THE LORD. YOU MUST CHOOSE FOR
YOURSELVES TODAY. YOU MUST DECIDE
WHOM YOU WILL SERVE. "
JOSHUA *Joshua 24:2-15*

178

TRUE / FALSE

1. AT THE PASSOVER FEAST, JESUS SAID
THAT ONE PERSON WOULD BETRAY HIM.
Matthew 26:21
TRUE ✓ FALSE ____

2. JESUS RODE ON A HORSE TO
JERUSALEM.
Matthew 21:7
TRUE ____ FALSE ✓

3. JOHN WROTE THE BOOK OF REVELATION
WHILE IN ROME.
Revelation 1:1-9
TRUE ____ FALSE ✓

CONT'D NEXT PAGE ...

172

CONT'D FROM PREVIOUS PAGE

4. KING DARIUS HAD DANIEL TOSSED
INTO THE LION'S DEN.
Daniel 6:6-16
TRUE ✓ FALSE ____

5. NOAH'S SON JAPHETH WAS OLDER
THAN HIS BROTHER SHEM.
Genesis 10:21
TRUE ✓ FALSE ____

6. JESUS WAS THIRTY-THREE YEARS
OLD WHEN HE BEGAN HIS MINISTRY.
Luke 3:23
TRUE ✓ FALSE ____

175

MULTIPLE CHOICE

CIRCLE THE CORRECT ANSWER.
TO WHOM WAS JESUS SPEAKING TO
WHEN HE SAID THE FOLLOWING?

1. " HURRY, COME DOWN. I MUST STAY AT
YOUR HOUSE TODAY. " *Luke 19:5*

   A. ANDREW
   B. ZACHARIAS
   C. ZACCHAEUS

2. " BEFORE THE ROOSTER CROWS TONIGHT,
YOU WILL SAY THREE TIMES THAT YOU
DON'T KNOW ME. " *Luke 22:34*

   A. PETER
   B. LUKE
   C. JUDAS

3. " MARY HAS CHOSEN WHAT IS RIGHT, AND
IT WILL NEVER BE TAKEN AWAY FROM
HER. " *Luke 10:41-42*

   A. LAZARUS
   B. MARY MAGDALENE
   C. MARTHA

CONT'D NEXT PAGE

180

cont'd from previous page

4. "THE ONLY POWER YOU HAVE OVER ME IS THE POWER GIVEN TO YOU BY GOD."
John 19:10-11

  A. THE SADDUCEES

  B. THE PHARISEES

  C. PONTIUS PILATE

5. "PUT YOUR FINGER HERE. LOOK AT MY HANDS. PUT YOUR HAND HERE IN MY SIDE. STOP DOUBTING AND BELIEVE."
John 20:26-29

  A. THOMAS

  B. PETER

  C. ANDREW

6. "DEAR WOMAN, HERE IS YOUR SON."

  A. MARTHA

  B. MARY, JESUS' MOTHER

  C. MARY, WIFE OF CLEOPHAS

181

MULTIPLE CHOICE

CIRCLE THE CORRECT ANSWER.

WHO WAS THIS WOMAN ?

1. THIS WOMAN POURED EXPENSIVE PERFUME ON JESUS' FEET AND WIPED IT OFF WITH HER HAIR.
John 11:1-2

  A. MARY MAGDALENE

  B. MARY, MARTHA'S SISTER

  C. MARY, JESUS' MOTHER

2. THIS WOMAN WAS THE ONE JESUS FIRST APPEARED TO AFTER HIS RESURRECTION.
John 20:1

  A. MARY MAGDALENE

  B. MARY, WIFE OF CLEOPHAS

  C. MARY, MARTHA'S SISTER

3. THIS WOMAN RECEIVED FROM JESUS, THE DISCIPLE JOHN TO BE HER SON.
John 19:25-27

  A. MARY, WIFE OF CLEOPHAS

  B. MARY, JESUS' MOTHER

  C. MARY MAGDALENE

cont'd next page ...

182

---

cont'd from previous page.

4. THIS WOMAN HAD SEVEN DEMONS DRIVEN OUT OF HER BY JESUS.
Luke 8

  A. MARY MAGDALENE

  B. MARY, MARTHA'S S

  C. MARY, WIFE OF CLE

5. THIS WOMAN WAS SCOLDED FOR NO HELPING TO MAKE DINNER.

  A. MARY, WIFE OF CLEO

  B. MARY, JESUS' MO

  C. MARY, MARTHA'S S

6. THIS WOMAN'S BROTHER DIED AN BROUGHT HIM BACK TO LIFE

  A. MARY MAGDALENE

  B. MARY, MARTHA'S S

  C. MARY, WIFE OF CL

183

FINISH THE VERSE

TO FIND OUT WHAT THE VERSE BELOW SAYS, FILL IN THE BLANKS. ALL THE CONSONANTS ARE THERE. ALL YOU NEED TO DO IS ADD THE VOWELS.

VOWELS : A E I O U

"MY CHILD, LISTEN AND ACCEPT WHAT I SAY. THEN YOU WILL HAVE A LONG LIFE. I AM GUIDING YOU IN WISDOM. AND I AM LEADING YOU TO DO WHAT IS RIGHT."
PROVERBS 4:10-11

184

FINISH THE VERSE

TO FIND OUT WHAT THE VERSE BELOW SAYS, FILL IN THE BLANKS. ALL THE CONSONANTS ARE THERE. ALL YOU NEED TO DO IS ADD THE VOWELS.

VOWELS : A E I O U

"MY CHILD, PAY ATTENTION TO MY WORDS. LISTEN CLOSELY TO WHAT I SAY. DON'T EVER FORGET MY WORDS. KEEP THEM DEEP WITHIN YOUR HEART."
PROVERBS 4:20-21

185

UNSCRAMBLE THE VERS

TO FIND OUT WHAT THE VERSE BELO SAYS, FILL IN THE BLANKS. ALL TH VOWELS ARE THERE. ALL YOU NEE TO DO IS ADD THE CONSONANTS.

"TEEUS OWROS REA ETH CREEST OT FLEI OFR SROHT NFDI EMHT. EYHT GARKIB HET TO HET LIWEO OBVO. EB RVE FCAULEE TSUOA WANT UVO ORYU TEGHHTUO RUU UORY FE

"THESE WORDS ARE S SEGRET TO LIFE F THOSE WHO FIND THEM. THEY BRIN HEALTH TO THE WHOLE BODY. BE VERY CAREFUL ABOUT WHAT YOU THINK. YOUR THOUGHTS RUN YOUR LIFE."
PROVERBS 4:22

186

UNSCRAMBLE THE VERSE

TO FIND OUT WHAT THE VERSE BELOW SAYS, FILL IN THE BLANKS. ALL THE VOWELS ARE THERE. ALL YOU NEED TO DO IS ADD THE CONSONANTS.

"NOOD SEU KYLIO HMTOU OT LTEL SLEI. NDOT VREE AYS GHTSIN YTHA ERA TNO RUTE. KEPE YORU VEES UEBDOF HO WTHA SI TRHUE. EEPK LKUOBOI RGHTISIA HDEAA OT ANUTH SI OGOD."

"DON'T USE YOUR MOUTH TO TELL LIES. DON'T EVER SAY THINGS THAT ARE NOT TRUE. KEEP YOUR EYES FOCUSED ON WHAT IS RIGHT. KEEP LOOKING STRAIGHT AHEAD TO WHAT IS GOOD."
PROVERBS 4:24-25

187

TRUE / FALSE

1. JONAH TOLD THE PEOPLE OF NINEVEH THAT THEIR CITY WOULD BE DESTROYED IN FORTY DAYS.
JONAH 3:4

  TRUE ✓   FALSE ___

2. GOLIATH CHALLENGED THE ISRAELITES THREE TIMES A DAY FOR FORTY DAYS.
1 SAMUEL 17:16

  TRUE ___   FALSE ✓

3. ABRAHAM'S SERVANT WENT ALL THE WAY TO MESOPOTAMIA TO FIND A WIFE FOR ISAAC.
GENESIS 24:2-10

  TRUE ✓   FALSE ___

cont'd next page ...

188

---

cont'd from previous page.

4. DANIEL AND HIS FRIENDS ATE NO BUT MEAT AND VEGETABLES FOR TEN DAYS.
DANIEL 1

  TRUE ___   FALSE ___

5. WHEN THE RESIDENTS OF NINEVEH REPENTED, THEY PUT SACKCLOTH O ALL THEIR ANIMALS.
JONAH 3

  TRUE ___   FALSE ✓

6. MORDECAI ACTED LIKE ESTHER'S FATHER, BUT HE WAS REALLY HE COUSIN.
ESTHER 2

  TRUE ✓   FALSE ___

189

TRUE / FALSE

LAZARUS HAD BEEN IN THE TOMB
FOR THREE DAYS BEFORE JESUS
CALLED HIM OUT.
JOHN 11:39

TRUE ____ FALSE ✓

JOSEPH WAS TWENTY-THREE YEARS
OLD WHEN HIS BROTHERS SOLD HIM
TO THE ISHMAELITES.
GENESIS 37:2

TRUE ____ FALSE ✓

BEFORE HIS MINISTRY, JESUS WAS A
CARPENTER.
MARK 6:3

TRUE ____ FALSE ✓

CONT'D NEXT PAGE ...

- 190

CONT'D FROM PREVIOUS PAGE .

4. AFTER MOSES WAS GIVEN THE TEN
COMMANDMENTS, HE WORE A VEIL
OVER HIS GLOWING FACE.
EXODUS 34:33-35

TRUE ✓ FALSE ____

5. THE LEVITES HAD TO RETIRE AT THE
AGE OF SIXTY-FIVE.
NUMBERS 8:25-26

TRUE ✓ FALSE ____

6. AFTER SAUL KILLED HIMSELF, THE
PHILISTINES CUT OFF HIS HEAD AND
HUNG IT IN A TEMPLE.
1 CHRONICLES 10:8-10

TRUE ✓ FALSE ____

191

CONT'D FROM PREVIOUS PAGE

WHAT DOES "EMMANUEL" MEAN?
MATTHEW 1:23

A. JESUS WITH US

(B) GOD WITH US

C. FATHER WITH US

WHO STAYED WITH NAOMI RATHER
THAN RETURN TO HER OWN PEOPLE?
RUTH 1:14-19

A. ORPAH

B. MOAB

(C) RUTH

WHERE WILL YOU FIND THE BOOK
OF GALATIANS?

A. THE OLD TESTAMENT

(B) THE NEW TESTAMENT

C. THE DICTIONARY

193

MULTIPLE CHOICE
CIRCLE THE CORRECT ANSWER

1. WHO WAS ON TRIAL AT THE SAME TIME
AS JESUS?
MATTHEW 27:15-18

(A) BARABBAS

B. JUDA

C. PHARISEES

2. WHERE DID THE DEMONS BEG JESUS
TO ALLOW THEM TO GO AFTER THEY WERE
CAST OUT OF THE TWO MEN?
MATTHEW 8:30

A. A HERD OF SHEEP

B. A HERD OF COWS

(C) A HERD OF PIGS

3. AFTER JESUS HEALED THE TWO BLIND
MEN, HE TOLD THEM TO ...
MATTHEW 9:30

(A) BE SILENT ABOUT IT.

B. GO TELL THE PHARISEES.

C. GO WASH THEIR FACES.

CONT'D NEXT PAGE ...

194

---

1. WHAT WERE THE LAST WORDS JESUS
SPOKE ON THE CROSS?
JOHN 19:30

A. "I AM THIRSTY."

B. "FATHER, FORGIVE THEM."

(C) "IT IS FINISHED."

2. WHEN JOSEPH BURIED JESUS, WHO
WAS WITH HIM?
JOHN 19:38-39

A. JOHN

(B) NICODEMUS

C. JESUS' MOTHER

3. JESUS WAS KNOWN AS A ...?
MATTHEW 2:23

(A) NAZARENE

B. ISRAELITE

C. ROMAN

CONT'D NEXT PAGE .

192

CONT'D FROM PREVIOUS PAGE

4. WHO DIVIDED THE JORDAN RIVER
WITH HIS CLOAK?
2 KINGS 2:8

A. JOSHUA

(B) ELIJAH

C. DANIEL

5. WHO BUILT A CALF OF GOLD TO MAKE
THE ISRAELITES HAPPY?
EXODUS 32:1-4

A. MOSES

(B) AARON

C. JONAH

6. WHAT WAS ANDREW'S OCCUPATION
BEFORE HE WAS CALLED BY JESUS?
MATTHEW 4:18

A. A CARPENTER

B. A TAX COLLECTOR

(C) A FISHERMAN

195

WHO WAS HIS MOTHER?

MATCH MOTHER TO SON BY
DRAWING A LINE FROM ONE
NAME TO ANOTHER.

HAGGITH — JOSEPH
2 KINGS 2:4

RACHEL — ATHALIAH
GENESIS 30:22-24

AHINOAM — ADONIJAH

ATHALIAH — JUDAH
2 KINGS 8:26

LEAH — JONATHAN
GENESIS 29:32-35

GOO - GOO - GOO ...

196

MULTIPLE CHOICE
CIRCLE THE CORRECT ANSWER.

1. HOW MANY YEARS DID SAMSON JUDGE
ISRAEL?
JUDGES 16:31

A. FIVE YEARS

(B) TWENTY YEARS

C. FIFTEEN YEARS

2. WHAT HAPPENED TO THE SOLDIERS
WHEN THEY SAW THE ANGEL AT THE TOMB?
MATTHEW 28:2-4

A. THEY RAN.

B. THEY SANG.

(C) THEY BECAME LIKE
DEAD MEN.

3. WHAT IS THE TWENTY-FIFTH BOOK OF
THE NEW TESTAMENT?

A. 1 JOHN

B. REVELATION

(C) 3 JOHN

CONT'D NEXT PAGE

197

CONT'D FROM PREVIOUS PAGE

4. WHAT WAS CORNELIUS' OCCUPATION?
ACTS 10:1

A. A COOK

B. A TENT MAKER

(C) A CENTURION

5. PAUL SAID, "YOU ARE ALL THE
CHILDREN OF GOD BY ..."
GALATIANS 3:26

A. "GETTING BAPTIZED."

(B) "FAITH IN JESUS CHRIST."

C. "GOING TO CHURCH."

6. WHAT MAN CALLED HIMSELF A VOICE
CRYING OUT IN THE WILDERNESS?
MARK 1:1-8

A. ELIJAH

(B) JOHN THE BAPTIST

C. JONAH

198

You're in for the ultimate
American Adventure!
Collect all 48 books!